D0756106

Russian
PHRASE BOOK & DICTIONARY

FOR SALE
80p

PRICE £1

HarperCollins*Publishers*

First published 1992

Copyright © HarperCollins Publishers
Published by HarperCollins Publishers
Printed in Hong Kong
ISBN 0 00-433972-X

INTRODUCTION

Your *Collins Phrase Book & Dictionary* is a handy, quick-reference guide that will help you make the most of your stay abroad. Its clear alphabetical layout will save you valuable time when you need that crucial word or phrase.

There are two main sections in this book:

  • 70 practical topics arranged in A-Z order from **ACCIDENTS** to **WINTER SPORTS** via such subjects as **BUYING**, **MENUS** and **TAXIS**. Each topic gives you the basic phrases you will need along with clear but simple pronunciation guidelines. In many cases, there's the added bonus of our 'Streetwise' travel tips – practical and often invaluable travel information. But be prepared – you are visiting a part of the world that is undergoing a period of change and rapid reform.
  And, if you've found the right phrase but still need a vital word, you're sure to find it in the final topic, **WORDS**, a brief but rigorously practical list of English words and their translations, chosen for their relevance to the needs of the general traveller.

  • A 2000-word foreign vocabulary; the key to all those mystifying but important notices, traffic signs, menus, etc which confront the traveller at every turn. This mini-dictionary will help you enjoy to the full the country's cuisine, save you time when asking directions, and perhaps prevent you getting into one or two tricky situations!

So, just flick through the pages to find the information you require. Why not start with a quick look at the **GRAMMAR**, **ALPHABET** and **PRONUNCIATION** topics? From there on the going is easy with your *Collins Phrase Book & Dictionary*.

Счастливого пути!

LIST OF TOPICS

Streetwise

*Most itineraries are pre-arranged through the State Tourist Board –
Intourist. If you break down or are involved in an accident, alert the
nearest Traffic Police Post* **ГАИ** *(ga-i). Help may not be instantly at
hand, so carry a warning triangle, fire extinguisher and first-aid kit.*

There's been an accident	**Случилась авария** *slu-chi-las' a-va-riya*
I've crashed my car	**Я разбил свою машину** *ya raz-bil sva-yu ma-schi-nu*
Please inform the police	**Сообщите в милицию, пожалуйста** *saap-shchi-ti vmi-li-tsiyu pa-zha-lusta*
I need a statement for my insurance	**Мне нужна справка для страховки** *mnye nuzh-na spraf-ka dlya stra-khof-ki*
He ran into me	**Он наехал на меня** *on na-ye-khal na mi-nya*
He was driving too fast	**Он ехал слишком быстро** *on ye-khal slisch-kam bis-tra*
He was too close	**Он был слишком близко** *on bil slisch-kam blis-ka*
He did not give way	**Он не пропустил меня** *on ni prapus-til mi-nya*
The car number was…	**Номер машины был…** *no-mir ma-schi-ni bil…*
He was coming from my right/left	**Он приближался ко мне справа/слева** *on pribli-zhal-sya ka mnye spra-va/slye-va*

See also **BREAKDOWNS, EMERGENCIES, TRAFFIC RULES**

ACCIDENTS – INJURIES

Streetwise

Under a reciprocal agreement with the UK, medical treatment is free of charge. Comprehensive travel insurance, including air ambulance service, is strongly recommended. If you have had an accident, inform the Intourist representative and your hotel Service Bureau immediately.

There's been an accident	**Случилась авария** *slu-**chi**-las' a-**va**-riya*
Call an ambulance/ a doctor	**Вызовите скорую/доктора** *vi-zaviti **sko**-ruyu/**dok**-tara*
He has hurt himself	**Он пострадал** *on pastra-**dal***
I am hurt	**Я пострадал(а)** *ya pastra-**dal**(a)*
He can't breathe/ move	**Он не может дышать/пошевелиться** *on ni **mo**-zhit di-**schat**'/paschivi-**lit**-sya*
I can't move my arm/leg	**Я не могу пошевелить рукой/ногой** *ya ni ma-**gu** paschivi-**lit**' ru-**koi**/na-**goi***
Cover him up	**Накройте его чем-нибудь** *na-**kroi**-ti ye-**vo** chyem-nibut'*
Don't move him	**Не двигайте его** *ni **dvi**-gaiti ye-**vo***
He has broken his arm/cut himself	**Он сломал руку/порезался** *on sla-**mal** ru-ku/pa-**rye**-zalsya*
I have had a fall	**Я упал(а)** *ya u-**pal**(a)*

See also **EMERGENCIES**

Streetwise

Whether travelling privately or with a group, accommodation arrangements must be made in advance, usually through the State Tourist Board – Intourist. The Intourist hotels have a Service Bureau with English-speaking staff. It might be wise to take a fit-all rubber plug, as these are sometimes missing.

I reserved a room in the name of…	**Я забронировал(а) комнату на имя…** *ya zabra-ni-raval(a) kom-natu na i-mya…*
What is my room number?	**Какой номер моей комнаты?** *ka-koi no-mir ma-yei kom-nati*
What floor is my room on?	**На каком этаже моя комната?** *na ka-kom ita-zhe ma-ya kom-nata*
I would like a room that is quiet	**Я хотел(а) бы тихую комнату** *ya kha-tyel(a) bi ti-khuyu kom-natu*
Could you have my luggage brought up?	**Вы можете поднести мой багаж?** *vi mo-zhiti padnis-ti moi ba-gasch*
What time is breakfast/dinner?	**Во сколько завтрак/ужин?** *va skol'-ka zaf-trak/u-zhin*
We will be staying for…days/one week	**Мы пробудем здесь…дня/неделю** *mi pra-bu-dim zdyes'…dnya/ni-dye-lyu*
I would like to speak to the manager	**Я хочу поговорить с администратором** *ya kha-chu pagava-rit' sadminis-tra-taram*

See also **HOTEL DESK, ROOM SERVICE**

Streetwise

If you are travelling independently, the English-speaking staff at your hotel Service Bureau will assist you in making or changing your reservations.

Where do I check in for the flight to London?	**Где регистрация рейса на Лондон?** *gdye rigis-**tra**-tsiya **ryei**-sa na **lon**-dan*
I'd like an aisle/ a window seat	**Я бы хотел(а) место в проходе/около окна** *ya bi kha-**tyel**(a) **myes**-ta fpra-**kho**-di/o-kala ak-**na***
Will a meal be served on the plane?	**Будут ли нас кормить в самолете?** *bu-dut li **nas** kar-**mit**' fsama-**luo**-ti*
Where is the snack bar/duty-free shop?	**Где буфет/беспошлинный магазин?** *gdye bu-**fyet**/bis-**posch**-linii maga-**zin***
Where can I change some money?	**Где я могу поменять деньги?** *gdye ya ma-**gu** pami-**nyat**' **dyen**'-gi*
Where do I get the bus to town?	**Откуда отходит автобус в город?** *at-**ku**-da at-**kho**-dit af-**to**-bus **vgo**-rat*
Where are the taxis/ telephones?	**Где такси/телефон?** *gdye tak-**si**/tili-**fon***
I want to hire a car	**Я хочу взять напрокат машину** *ya kha-**chu** vzyat' napra-**kat** ma-**schi**-nu*
I am being met	**Меня встречают** *mi-**nya** fstri-**cha**-yut*

The Cyrillic alphabet is a modified version of the Greek alphabet and has 33 letters. It is worth spending some time learning the letters before you arrive; it will help you recognize names and make you feel more confident.

LETTER	SOUNDS LIKE	LETTER	SOUNDS LIKE
а А (unstressed)	a in car a in aloud	р Р	r in arrow (rolled)
б Б	b in bed	с С	ss in miss
в В	v in voice	т Т	t in take
г Г	g in good	у У	oo in cool
д Д	d in dog	ф Ф	f in fat
е Е	ye in yes	х Х	ch in loch
ё Ё	yo in yore	ц Ц	ts in its
ж Ж	s in pleasure	ч Ч	ch in cheese
з З	z in zoo	ш Ш	sh in shun
и И	ee in need	щ Щ	shch in fresh cheese
й Й	y in you	ъ (hard sign) not pronounced but suggests slight separation from next letter	
к К	k in king		
л Л	l in league (soft) l in gold (hard)	ы	y in fairy
м М	m in map (hard) m in mean (soft)	ь (soft sign) not pronounced; softens the preceding consonant	
н Н	n in now	э Э	e in egg
о О (unstressed)	o in ore a in aloud	ю Ю	u in use
п П	p in pen	я Я	ya in yarn

See also **GRAMMAR, PRONUNCIATION**

ASKING QUESTIONS

Streetwise

Like French, Russian has two forms of the pronoun you: **ты** (**ti**) *the familiar form, and* **вы** (**vi**) *the polite form which we have used in this book. You should address a man as* **господин** (gaspa-**din**), *a woman as* **госпожа** (gaspa-**zha**) *and an unmarried or young woman as* **девушка** (**dye**-vuschka). *However, the words 'Sir', 'Madam' and 'Miss' will be understood.*

Is it far/expensive?	**Это далеко/дорого?** *e*-ta dali-**ko**/**do**-raga
Do you understand?	**Вы понимаете?** *vi* pani-**ma**-yeti
Can you help me?	**Вы можете мне помочь?** *vi* **mo**-zhiti **mnye** pa-**moch**
Where are the toilets?	**Где туалет?** *gdye* tua-**lyet**
How do I get there?	**Как мне туда добраться?** *kak* mnye tu-**da** da-**brat**-sa
How far is it to…?	**Как далеко до…?** *kak* dali-**ko** da…
Is there a good restaurant?	**Там есть хороший ресторан?** *tam* **yest'** kha-**ro**-schii rista-**ran**
What is this?	**Что это?** *schto* **e**-ta
How much is it?	**Сколько это стоит?** *skol'*-ka **e**-ta **sto**-it
How many kilometres?	**Сколько километров?** *skol'*-ka kila-**myet**-raf

See also **CONVERSATION, GREETINGS**

Streetwise

Where bathing is forbidden you will see the sign **не купаться!** *or* **купание запрещено!**

Is it safe to swim here?	**Здесь безопасно купаться?** *zdyes' byeza-pas-na ku-pat-sa*
When is high/low tide?	**Когда прилив/отлив?** *kag-da pri-lif/at-lif*
Is the water deep?	**Здесь глубоко?** *zdyes' gluba-ko*
Are there strong currents?	**Здесь сильное течение?** *zdyes' sil'-naye ti-chye-niye*
Is it a private/quiet beach?	**Это частный/тихий пляж?** *e-ta chas-nii/ti-khii plyasch*
Where do we change?	**Где можно переодеться?** *gdye mozh-na piria-dyet-sa*
Can I hire a deckchair/boat?	**Можно ли взять напрокат шезлонг/ лодку?** *mozh-na li vzyat' napra-kat schiz-lonk/lot-ku*
Can I go fishing/ windsurfing?	**Здесь можно ловить рыбу/заниматься винд-серфингом?** *zdyes' mozh-na la-vit' ri-bu/zani-mat-sa vint-ser-fingam*
Is there a children's pool?	**Там есть бассейн для детей?** *tam yest' ba-sein dlya di-tyei*
Where can I get an ice cream?	**Где продается мороженое?** *gdye prada-yot-sa ma-ro-zhinaye*

BREAKDOWNS

If you break down along the highway, you must alert the nearest Traffic Police Post ГАИ (ga-i). Repairs are carried out at Service Stations (look for the sign of the spanner). There are auto-inspection ramps at lay-bys for DIY repairs. Spare parts are in short supply, particularly for foreign makes, so take your own, and carry a jerrycan and spare oil.

My car has broken down	**Моя машина сломалась** ma-**ya** ma-**schi**-na sla-**ma**-las'
Something is wrong with the brakes	**Что-то не в порядке с тормозами** **schto**-ta nifpa-**ryat**-ki starma-**za**-mi
I have run out of petrol	**У меня кончился бензин** umi-**nya kon**-chilsya bin-**zin**
There's a leak in the petrol tank/radiator	**Бензобак/радиатор протекает** binza-**bak**/radi-**a**-tar prati-**ka**-yet
The engine is overheating	**Мотор перегревается** ma-**tor** pirigri-**va**-yetsa
Can you tow me to a garage?	**Вы можете отбуксировать меня в гараж?** vi **mo**-zhiti atbuk-**si**-ravat' mi-**nya** vga-**rasch**
Can you send a mechanic/a breakdown van?	**Вы можете прислать механика/техпомощь?** vi **mo**-zhiti pri-**slat'** mi-**kha**-nika/tyekh-**po**-mashch
Do you have the parts?	**У вас есть запчасти?** uvas **yest'** zap-**chas**-ti
The windscreen has shattered	**Ветровое стекло разбито** vyetra-**vo**-ye sti-**klo** raz-**bi**-ta

See also **EMERGENCIES, TRAFFIC RULES**

I have an appointment with…	**У меня встреча с…** *umi-**nya** fstrye-cha s…*
He is expecting me	**Он меня ждёт** *on mi-**nya** zhdyot*
Can I leave a message with his secretary?	**Могу я оставить записку с секретарем?** *ma-**gu** ya as-**ta**-vit' za-**pi**-sku ssikrita-**ryom***
I am free tomorrow morning/for lunch	**Я свободен/свободна завтра утром/в обед** *ya sva-**bo**-din/sva-**bod**-na zaf-tra u-tram/va-**byet***
Here is my business card	**Вот моя визитная карточка** *vot ma-**ya** vi-**zit**-naya **kar**-tachka*
Can I send a telex from here?	**Могу я послать отсюда телекс?** *ma-**gu** ya pa-**slat'** at-**syu**-da **tye**-liks*
Where can I get some photocopying done?	**Где я могу сделать фотокопии?** *gdye ya ma-**gu** zdye-lat' fota-**ko**-pii*
I want to send this by courier	**Я хочу послать это с курьером** *ya kha-**chu** pa-**slat'** e-ta skur-**ye**-ram*
I will send you further details/a sample	**Я вышлю вам дальнейшие подробности/образцы** *ya **vi**-schlu **vam** dal'-**nei**-schii pa-**drob**-nasti/abras-tsi*
Have you a catalogue/some literature?	**У вас есть каталог/какая-нибудь литература?** *uvas **yest'** kata-**lok**/ka-**ka**-yanibut' litira-**tu**-ra*
I'm going to the trade fair/the exhibition	**Я собираюсь на ярмарку/выставку** *ya sabi-**ra**-yus' na **yar**-marku/**vi**-stafku*

BUYING

Streetwise

Apart from the airport duty-free shops, duty-paid shops run in conjunction with Aer Rianta Int. can be found in some ot the large St Petersburg hotels. The Russian-state 'Beriozka' foreign currency shop chain is in decline as more and more souvenirs are on sale for roubles. In department stores, first you choose the item and find out the price. You then go to pay at the cash desk **касса** *(ka-sa), returning with the receipt to collect your purchase. Ask the salesperson to write down the price if you are unsure. Take your own carrier bag, as these are not provided.*

Please show that to me	**Покажите мне это, пожалуйста** *paka-zhi-ti mnye e-ta pa-zha-lusta*
How much is that?	**Сколько это стоит?** *skol'-ka e-ta sto-it*
Do you have another one?	**У вас есть еще?** *uvas yest' ye-shcho*
Please write down the price	**Напишите цену, пожалуйста** *napi-schi-ti tse-nu pa-zha-lusta*
I'd like a newspaper/ some apples	**Мне нужна газета/несколько яблок** *mnye nuzh-na ga-zye-ta/nyes-kal'ka yab-lak*
Have you got any bread/matches?	**У вас есть хлеб/спички?** *uvas yest' khlyep/spich-ki*
Please wrap it up	**Заверните, пожалуйста** *zavir-ni-ti pa-zha-lusta*

THE SALESPERSON MAY SAY:

Платите в кассу *pla-ti-ti fkas-su*	Pay at the cash desk

See also **PAYING, SHOPPING**

Streetwise

Camp sites are open from June to October, but you must arrange your itinerary and overnight stops in advance through Intourist. You can either rent space for your tent or rent a tent or hut. Facilities can be very basic.

We are looking for the camp site	**Мы ищем кемпинг** *mi **i**-shchim **kyem**-pink*
We have booked in advance	**Мы заказали заранее** ***mi** zaka-**za**-li za-**ra**-niye*
My name is…	**Меня зовут…** *mi-**nya** za-**vut**…*
We want to stay one night	**Мы хотим остановиться на одну ночь** ***mi** kha-**tim** astana-**vit**-sa na ad-**nu** noch*
Can we rent a tent/ hut?	**Мы можем взять напрокат палатку/ домик?** *mi **mo**-zhim vzyat' napra-**kat** pa-**lat**-ku/**do**-mik*
Is there a shop/ restaurant on the site?	**В кемпинге есть магазин/ресторан?** *fkyem-pingi yest' maga-**zin**/rista-**ran***
Where is the washroom/drinking water?	**Где уборная/питьевая вода?** *gdye u-**bor**-naya/pitye-**va**-ya va-**da***
What facilities do you have on the site?	**Какие удобства у вас есть в кемпинге?** *ka-**ki**-ye u-**dop**-stva u vas **yest' fkyem**-pingye*
Is there electricity?	**Электричество есть?** *elik-**tri**-chistva **yest'***

CAR HIRE

Streetwise

Intourist can arrange for the hire of a car and there are now new joint ventures specializing in the hire of foreign cars. You should enquire at the hotel Service Bureau. It is still more common to hire a car along with the services of a driver.

I want to hire a car	**Я хочу взять напрокат машину** *ya kha-**chu** vzyat' napra-**kat** ma-**schi**-nu*
I need a car with a chauffeur	**Мне нужна машина с шофером** *mnye nuzh-**na** ma-**schi**-na s scha-**fyo**-ram*
I want a large/small car	**Мне нужна большая/маленькая машина** *mnye nuzh-**na** bal'-**scha**-ya/ma-**lin**'kaya ma-**schi**-na*
Is there a charge per kilometre?	**Есть ли тариф за километр?** *yest'li ta-**rif** zakila-**myetr** *
What is the hourly/daily charge?	**Какой тариф за час/за день?** *ka-**koi** ta-**rif** za **chas**/za **dyen**' *
My husband/my wife will be driving as well	**Мой муж/моя жена тоже будет вести машину** *moi **musch**/ma-**ya** zhi-**na to**-zhe **bu**-dit vis-**ti** ma-**schi**-nu*
Is there a radio/radio-cassette?	**Там есть радио/магнитофон?** *tam **yest**' **ra**-dio/magnita-**fon** *
How do I operate the controls?	**Как работает эта машина?** *kak ra-**bo**-tait e-ta ma-**schi**-na*
Please explain the car documents	**Объясните, пожалуйста, документы на машину** *abyes-**ni**-ti pa-**zha**-lusta daku-**myen**-ti nama-**schi**-nu*

See also **BREAKDOWNS, EMERGENCIES, PETROL STATION, TRAFFIC RULES**

CELEBRATIONS

Streetwise

Christmas and Easter are observed according to the Russian Orthodox Church, shortly after we would normally celebrate them. New Year **Новый Год** (**no**-vii **got**) *on 1 January is when the main festivities take place with a fir tree and small gift for children. Adults celebrate with a good meal, which only begins once they have toasted in the New Year with champagne, and which can often last till dawn.*

When are the local festivals?	**Когда местные праздники?** kag-**da** myes-nii **praz**-niki
Happy birthday!	**С Днем Рождения!** **zdnyom** razh-**dye**-niya
Merry Christmas!	**С Рождеством!** srazhdist-**vom**
Happy New Year!	**С Новым Годом!** **sno**-vim **go**-dam
Congratulations!	**Поздравляем!** pazdrav-**lya**-yem
Best wishes for…!	**Наилучшие пожелания…!** nai-**lut**-schii pazhi-**la**-niya…
Have a good time!	**Всего хорошего!** fsye-**vo** kha-**ro**-schiva
Cheers!	**Будьте здоровы!** **but'**-ti zda-**ro**-vi
Enjoy your meal!	**Приятного аппетита!** pri-**yat**-nava api-**ti**-ta

CHEMIST'S

Streetwise

The name for a chemist's is **аптека** (ap-**tye**-ka). *They may not have a large selection of medicines because of shortages, and although most hotels have a stand selling a range of basic medicines, you are advised to take your own brands from home.*

I want something for a headache/a sore throat/toothache	**Мне нужно что-нибудь от головной боли/для горла/от зубной боли** mnye **nuzh**-na **schto**-nibyt' at galav-**noi bo**-li/dlya **gor**-la/adzyb-**noi bo**-li
I would like some aspirin/sticking plaster	**Мне нужен аспирин/пластырь** mnye **nu**-zhin aspi-**rin/plas**-tir'
Have you anything for insect bites/diarrhoea?	**У вас есть что-нибудь от укусов насекомых/поноса?** uvas **yest'** **schto**-nibut' atu-**ku**-saf nasi-**ko**-mikh/pa-**no**-sa
I have a cold/a cough	**У меня простуда/кашель** umi-**nya** pra-**stu**-da/**ka**-schel'
Is this suitable for an upset stomach/hay fever?	**Это подходит от расстройства желудка/сенной лихорадаки?** e-ta pat-**kho**-dit at ras-**troi**-stva zhi-**lut**-ka/sin-**noi** likha-**rat**-ki
How much/many do I take?	**По сколько мне принимать?** pa **skol'**-ka **mnye** prini-**mat'**
How often do I take it?	**Сколько раз в день принимать?** **skol'**-ka **raz** vdyen' prini-**mat'**
Is it safe for children?	**Это безопасно для детей?** e-ta biza-**pas**-na dlya di-**tyei**

See also **BUYING, PAYING**

Streetwise

Children are warmly welcomed. They can also be an effective way of breaking down language barriers. Look out for puppet theatres: an ideal way of entertaining both children and adults.

I have two children	**У меня двое детей** *umi-nya dvo-ye di-tyei*
Could we have adjoining rooms?	**Мы бы хотели смежные комнаты** *mi bi kha-tye-li smyezh-nii kom-nati*
Do you have facilities for children?	**У вас есть удобства для детей?** *uvas yest' u-dop-stva dlya di-tyei*
Have you got a cot for the baby?	**У вас есть детская кроватка?** *uvas yest' dyets-kaya kra-vat-ka*
Where can I feed/change the baby?	**Где я могу покормить/перепеленать ребенка?** *gdye ya ma-gu pakar-mit'/piripili-nat' ri-byon-ka*
Where can I warm the baby's bottle?	**Где можно подогреть детский рожок?** *gdye mozh-na pada-gryet' dets-kii ra-zhok*
Is there a playroom for children?	**У вас есть игровая комната для детей?** *uvas yest' igra-va-ya kom-nata dlya di-tyei*
Is there a baby-sitting service?	**Можно нанять няню?** *mozh-na na-nyat' nya-nyu*
My son is six years old	**Моему сыну шесть лет** *maye-mu si-nu schest' lyet*

See also **ENTERTAINMENT**

CHURCH AND WORSHIP

Streetwise

Religions vary according to the region, but the main ones are Russian Orthodox and Muslim. Many church buildings have been returned to believers and reopened for worship. Visitors should be suitably dressed and avoid shorts, short skirts and bare shoulders. Be warned: if you are planning to attend a service, there are no pews or seats!

Is it possible to visit the church?	**Можно посетить церковь?** *mozh-na pasi-tit' tser-kaf'*
Is there a Protestant/ Catholic church?	**Здесь есть протестантская/ католическая церковь?** *zdyes' yest' pratis-tans-kaya/kata-li-chiskaya tser-kaf*
What time is the service?	**Во сколько начинается служба?** *va skol'-ka nachi-na-itsa sluzh-ba*
How long is the service?	**Сколько длится служба?** *skol'-ka dlit-sa sluzh-ba*
Can we visit the mosque/synagogue	**Можна зайти в мечеть/ в синагогу?** *mozh-na zai-ti vmi-chyet'/fsina-go-gu*
I am Protestant/ Catholic/Jewish	**Я протестант/католик/иудей** *ya pratis-tant/ka-to-lik/iu-dyei*

CITY TRAVEL – BUS & TRAM

Streetwise

*Buses (A), trolleybuses (T) and trams (T) run from 0600 to 0100.
Tickets cost a modest flat rate and can be bought from street kiosks. You
must validate your ticket on board, and it is normal for passengers to
pass their tickets forward to the ticket punch machine, particularly
during peak times when it can be very crowded.*

A book of tickets, please	**Книжечку талонов, пожалуйста** *kni-zhichku ta-lo-naf pa-zha-lusta*
Which number goes to the centre/hotel?	**Какой номер идет в центр/к гостинице?** *ka-koi no-mir i-dyot ftsentr/kgas-ti-nitse*
Where is the stop for bus/trolleybus/tram number…?	**Где остановка автобуса/троллейбуса/ трамвая номер…?** *gdye asta-nof-ka af-to-busa/tra-lyei-busa/ tram-va-ya no-mir…*
Please pass my ticket along	**Передайте билет, пожалуйста** *piri-dai-tye bi-lyet pa-zha-lusta*
Is this the right stop for…?	**Это правильная остановка для…?** *e-ta pra-vil'naya asta-nof-ka dlya…*
Please tell me when to get off	**Подскажите, пожалуйста, когда мне выходить** *patska-zhi-tye pa-zha-lusta kag-da mnye vikha-dit'*
Please let me through	**Пропустите, пожалуйста** *prapus-ti-tye pa-zha-lusta*
Does this bus/ trolleybus/tram go to the centre?	**Этот автобус/троллейбус/трамвай идет в центр?** *e-tat af-to-bus/tra-lyei-bus/tram-vai i-dyot ftsentr*

See also **CITY TRAVEL – METRO**

Streetwise

*Most large cities have a metro system (**M**). The Moscow and St Petersburg Metros are renowned for cleanliness, punctuality and the splendid decor of some of their stations. They run from 0600 to 0130 daily and a modest flat rate gives you unlimited travel. The only maps of the system are at the entrance and in the carriages, so plan your journey before entering. On the train the name of the station and then the next stop are announced automatically. If in doubt, count the number of stops to your destination.*

Where is the nearest Metro station?	**Где ближайшая станция метро?** *gdye bli-**zhai**-schaya **stan**-tsiya mi-**tro***
How can I get to the nearest Metro station?	**Как дойти до ближайшей станции метро?** *kak dai-ti da bli-**zhai**-schii **stan**-tsii mi-**tro***
Is this train going to the centre?	**Этот поезд идет в центр?** *e-tat **po**-ist i-**dyot** ftsentr*
Which station is this?	**Какая это станция?** *ka-**ka**-ya **e**-ta **stan**-tsiya*
Which is the next station?	**Какая следующая станция?** *ka-**ka**-ya **slye**-dushchaya **stan**-tsiya*
Where do I change for…?	**Где мне сделать пересадку…?** *gdye mnye **zdye**-lat' piri-**sat**-ku…*

YOU WILL HEAR:

Осторожно! Двери закрываются! *asta-**rozh**-na **dvye**-ri zakri-**va**-yutsa*	Watch out! The doors are closing
Следующая остановка… *slye-dushchaya asta-**nof**-ka…*	The next stop is…

Streetwise

Laundry is taken care of by the attendant **дежурная** *(di-**zhur**-naya) on your hotel floor, or by the maid. Service can be lengthy, so take some travel soap. An ironing room is usually available.*

Is there a laundry service?	**Можно сдать белье в стирку?** *mozh-na **zdat'** bil-yo fstir-ku*
Is there a Launderette/ dry cleaner's nearby?	**Есть ли рядом прачечная/химчистка?** *yest' li **rya**-dam **pra**-chichnaya/khim-**chist**-ka*
Where can I get this skirt cleaned/ ironed?	**Где можно почистить/погладить юбку?** *gdye **mozh**-na pa-**chis**-tit'/pa-**gla**-dit' **yup**-ku*
Could you clean/ mend this?	**Вы можете почистить/починить это?** *vi **mo**-zhiti pa-**chis**-tit'/pachi-**nit** e-ta*
Where can I do some washing?	**Где я могу постирать?** *gdye ya ma-**gu** pasti-**rat'***
I need some soap and hot water	**Мне нужно мыло и горячая вода** *mnye **nuzh**-na **mi**-lo i ga-**rya**-chaya va-**da***
Where can I dry my clothes?	**Где можно высушить одежду?** *gdye **mozh**-na **vi**-suschit' a-**dyezh**-du*
Can you remove this stain?	**Вы можете вывести это пятно?** *vi **mo**-zhiti **vi**-visti e-ta pit-**no***
This fabric is very delicate	**Это очень тонкая ткань** *e-ta o-chin' **ton**-kaya **tkan'***
When will my things be ready?	**Когда будут готовы мои вещи?** *kag-**da bu**-dut ga-**to**-vi mai **vye**-shchi*

See also **ROOM SERVICE**

CLOTHES

Streetwise

Supplies can be erratic in local shops and if you see something you like, buy it straight away. Fur hats, coats and scarves are always a popular buy.

Can you measure me, please?	**Вы можете снять с меня мерки?** *vi* **mo**-*zhiti* **snyat'** *smi-***nya** *myer-ki*
May I try this on?	**Можно мне примерить это?** ***mozh****-na mnye pri-****mye****-rit'* **e***-ta*
May I take it over to the light?	**Можно я посмотрю на свету?** ***mozh****-na* **ya** *pasmat-****ryu*** *nasvi-****tu***
Where are the changing rooms?	**Где примерочные?** ***gdye*** *pri-****mye****-rachnii*
Is there a mirror?	**Здесь есть зеркало?** *zdyes'* **yest'** **zyer***-kala*
It's too big/small	**Слишком большой/маленький** *slisch-kam bal'-****schoi****/ma-linkii*
What is the material?	**Какой это материал?** *ka-****koi*** *e-****ta*** *matir'-****yal***
Is it washable?	**Это можно стирать?** *e-ta* ***mozh****-na sti-****rat'***
I don't like it	**Мне это не нравится** *mnye* **e***-ta ni* **nra***-vitsa*
I don't like the colour	**Мне не нравится цвет** *mnye ni* **nra***-vitsa tsvyet*

See also **BUYING, PAYING, SHOPPING**

Streetwise

Complaints should be made directly to the Intourist representative who will deal with any problems.

This does not work	**Это не работает** *e-ta ni ra-bo-tait*
I can't turn the heating off/on	**Я не могу выключить/включить отопление** *ya ni ma-gu vi-klyuchit'/fklyu-chit' ata-plye-niye*
The lights don't work	**Свет не работает** *svyet ni ra-bo-tait*
I can't open the window	**Я не могу открыть окно** *ya nima-gu at-krit' a-kno*
The toilet won't flush	**Туалет не смывает** *tua-lyet nismi-va-it*
There is no hot water/ toilet paper	**Здесь нет горячей воды/туалетной бумаги** *zdyes' nyet ga-rya-chii va-di/tua-lyet-nai bu-ma-gi*
The washbasin is dirty	**Раковина грязная** *ra-kavina gryaz-naya*
There's no plug in the bath/wash basin	**В ванне/раковине нет пробки** *v van-ye/ra-kavinye nyet prop-ki*
The room is noisy	**Комната шумная** *kom-nata schum-naya*
We are still waiting to be served	**Нас все еще не обслужили** *nas fsyo ye-shcho ni apslu-zhi-li*
I bought this here yesterday	**Я купил(а) это здесь вчера** *ya ku-pil(a) e-ta zdyes' fchi-ra*

CONVERSATION

Streetwise

Russians have three names: a first name, a patronymic (i.e. father's name) and surname. In formal situations a person will be introduced by their first name and patronymic; thus instead of Anton Pavlovich Checkhov being introduced as Anton Checkhov, he would be introduced as Anton Pavlovich. It is customary to shake hands on both meeting and parting. Kissing is for family and close friends.

How do you do?	**Здравствуйте!** *zdrast-vuitye*
Hello	**Привет** *pri-vyet*
Goodbye	**До свидания** *dasvi-da-niya*
Do you speak English?	**Вы говорите по-английски?** *vi gava-ri-tye paan-glis-ki*
I don't speak Russian	**Я не говорю по-русски** *ya ni gava-ryu pa-rus-ki*
What's your name?	**Как вас зовут?** *kak vas za-vut*
My name is…	**Меня зовут…** *mi-nya za-vut…*
I'm English/Scottish/Welsh	**Я из Англии/Шотландии/Уэльса** *ya iz an-glii/schat-lan-dii/uel-sa*
Whereabouts are you from?	**Откуда вы родом?** *at-ku-da vi ro-dam*
Would you like to come out with me?	**Вы хотите пойти погулять со мной?** *vi kha-ti-ti pai-ti pagu-lyat' sa mnoi*

CONVERSATION

Yes, please

Да, спасибо
da spa-*si*-ba

No, thank you

Нет, спасибо
nyet spa-*si*-ba

Thank you very much

Спасибо большое
spa-*si*-ba bal'-*scho*-ye

Don't mention it

Не за что
nye-zaschto

I'm sorry

Извините
izvi-*ni*-tye

I'm on holiday here

Я здесь отдыхаю
ya zdyes' atdi-*kha*-yu

This is my first trip
to…

Это моя первая поездка в…
e-ta ma-*ya per*-vaya pa-*yest*-ka v…

Do you mind if I
smoke?

Вы не возражаете, если я закурю?
vi ni vazra-*zha*-yeti *yes*-li ya zaku-*ryu*

Would you like a
drink?

Хотите что-нибудь выпить?
kha-*ti*-tye *schto*-nibut' *vi*-pit'

Have you ever been
to Britain?

Вы были когда-нибудь в Англии?
vi *bi*-li kag-*da*-nibut' *van*-glii

Did you like it there?

Вам там понравилось?
vam tam pa-*nra*-vilas'

See also **ASKING QUESTIONS, GREETINGS**

CONVERSION CHARTS

In the weight and length charts, the middle figure can be either metric or imperial. Thus 3.3 feet = 1 metre, 1 foot = 0.3 metres, and so on.

feet		metres	inches		cm	lbs		kg
3.3	1	0.3	0.39	1	2.54	2.2	1	0.45
6.6	2	0.61	0.79	2	5.08	4.4	2	0.91
9.9	3	0.91	1.18	3	7.62	6.6	3	1.4
13.1	4	1.22	1.57	4	10.6	8.8	4	1.8
16.4	5	1.52	1.97	5	12.7	11	5	2.2
19.7	6	1.83	2.36	6	15.2	13.2	6	2.7
23	7	2.13	2.76	7	17.8	15.4	7	3.2
26.2	8	2.44	3.15	8	20.3	17.6	8	3.6
29.5	9	2.74	3.54	9	22.9	19.8	9	4.1
32.9	10	3.05	3.9	10	25.4	22	10	4.5
			4.3	11	27.9			
			4.7	12	30.1			

°C	0	5	10	15	17	20	22	24	26	28	30	35	37	38	40	50	100
°F	32	41	50	59	63	68	72	75	79	82	86	95	98.4	100	104	122	212

Km	10	20	30	40	50	60	70	80	90	100	110	120
Miles	6.2	12.4	18.6	24.9	31	37.3	43.5	49.7	56	62	68.3	74.6

Tyre pressures

lb/sq in	15	18	20	22	24	26	28	30	33	35
kg/sq cm	1.1	1.3	1.4	1.5	1.7	1.8	2	2.1	2.3	2.5

Liquids

gallons	1.1	2.2	3.3	4.4	5.5
litres	5	10	15	20	25

pints	0.44	0.88	1.76
litres	0.25	0.5	1

See also MEASUREMENTS, NUMBERS

CUSTOMS AND PASSPORTS

Streetwise

You will require a visa which can be arranged through your travel agent or through Intourist in the UK. On arrival you fill out a customs declaration form listing your money and valuables. Be sure to present it each time you change money. This form has to be handed in to the Customs Inspector on departure, together with a newly completed form.

I need a customs declaration form in English	**Мне нужна декларация на английском** *mnye nuzh-**na** dikla-**ra**-tsiya naan-**glis**-kam*
I have nothing to declare	**Мне нечего декларировать** *mnye **nye**-chiva dikla-**ri**-ravat'*
My wife/husband and I have a joint passport	**У нас с женой/мужем один паспорт** *u **nas** s zhi-**noi**/**mu**-zhyem a-**din pas**-part*
The children are on this passport	**Дети в этом паспорте** ***dye**-ti **ve**-tam **pas**-parti*
I am a British national	**Я из Великобритании** *ya iz vyelikabri-**ta**-nii*
We are here on holiday	**Мы здесь отдыхаем** *mi zdyes' atdi-**kha**-yem*
I am here on business	**Я здесь по делам** *ya zdyes' padi-**lam***
It is a present	**Это подарок** *e-ta pa-**da**-rak*
I shall be staying two weeks	**Я остановлюсь на две недели** *ya astanav-**lyus'** na **dvye** ni-**dye**-li*

DATES AND CALENDAR

What's the date today?	Какое сегодня число?	ka-**ko**-ye si-**vod**-nya chi-**slo**
Today is November 7th	Сегодня седьмое ноября	si-**vod**-nya sid'-**mo**-ye nayab-**rya**
We will be there on the 3rd of May 1992	Мы будем там третьего мая девяноста второго года	**mi** bu-**dim** tam **trye**-tiva **ma**-ya divi-**no**-sta fta-**ro**-va **go**-da

Monday	понедельник	pani-**dyel'**-nik
Tuesday	вторник	**ftor**-nik
Wednesday	среда	sri-**da**
Thursday	четверг	chit-**vyerk**
Friday	пятница	**pyat**-nitsa
Saturday	суббота	su-**bo**-ta
Sunday	воскресенье	vaskri-**syen**-ye

January	январь	yen-**var'**
February	февраль	fi-**vral'**
March	март	**mart**
April	апрель	a-**pryel'**
May	май	**mai**
June	июнь	i-**yun'**
July	июль	i-**yul'**
August	август	**av**-gust
September	сентябрь	sin-**tyabr'**
October	октябрь	ak-t**yabr'**
November	ноябрь	na-**yabr'**
December	декабрь	di-**kabr'**

Streetwise

Dental treatment is free, but overall standards are not very high. The Intourist representative or the hotel Service Bureau will help if you do need to see a dentist urgently.

I need to see the dentist (urgently)	**Мне (срочно) нужно к дантисту** *mnye (sroch-na) nuzh-na k dan-tis-tu*
I have toothache	**У меня болит зуб** *umi-nya ba-lit zup*
I've broken a tooth	**Я сломал(а) зуб** *ya sla-mal(a) zup*
A filling has come out	**У меня выпала пломба** *umi-nya vi-pala plom-ba*
My gums are bleeding/ are sore	**У меня кровоточат/болят десны** *umi-nya krava-to-chat/ba-lyat dyos-ni*
Can you fix it?	**Вы можете это сделать?** *vi mo-zhiti e-ta zdye-lat'*
My dentures need repairing	**Мне нужно починить протезы** *mnye nuzh-na pachi-nit' pra-tye-zi*

THE DENTIST MAY SAY:

Мне придется его удалить *mnye pri-dyot-sa ye-vo uda-lit'*	I shall have to take it out
Вам нужна пломба *vam nuzh-na plom-ba*	You need a filling
Сейчас может быть больно *si-chas mo-zhit bit' bol'-na*	This might hurt a bit

DIRECTIONS

Streetwise

Jay-walking is forbidden on pain of an on-the-spot fine. Cross the road either by subway **подземный переход** *(pad-zyem-nii piri-khot) or at a zebra crossing. Be careful: cars are not obliged to stop for pedestrians.*

Where is the nearest post office?	**Где ближайшая почта?** *gdye bli-zhai-schaya poch-ta*
How do I get to the airport?	**Как мне проехать в аэропорт?** *kak mnye pra-ye-khat' vaero-port*
Is this the right way to the cathedral?	**Это верный путь к собору?** *e-ta vyer-nii put' ksa-bo-ru*
I am looking for the tourist information office	**Я ищу турбюро** *ya i-shchu turbyu-ro*
Is it far to walk/ by car?	**Это далеко пешком/на машине?** *e-ta dali-ko pisch-kom/nama-schi-nye*
Which road do I take for...?	**Какая дорога ведет к...?** *ka-ka-ya da-ro-ga vi-dyot k...*
Is this the turning for...?	**Это поворот на...?** *e-ta pava-rot na...*
How do I get to the main road?	**Как добраться до главной дороги?** *kak da-brat-sa da glav-nai da-ro-gi*
I have lost my way	**Я потерялся(потерялась)** *ya pati-ryal-sa(pati-rya-las')*
Can you show me on the map?	**Вы можете показать мне по карте?** *vi mo-zhiti paka-zat' mnye pa kar-tye*

Streetwise

Under a reciprocal agreement with the UK, medical treatment is free, but standards vary and medicines may be in short supply. If you feel unwell, notify the hotel Service Bureau or the Intourist representative and they will arrange for a doctor to call.

I need a doctor	**Мне нужен врач** *mnye **nu**-zhin **vrach***
Can I make an appointment with the doctor?	**Можно записаться на прием к врачу?** ***mozh**-na zapi-**sat**-sa na pri-**yom** kvra-**chu***
My son/my wife is ill	**Мой сын/моя жена заболел(а)** *moi **sin**/ma-**ya** zhi-**na** zabal-**lyel**(a)*
I have a sore throat/ a stomach upset	**У меня болит горло/расстроен желудок** *umi-**nya** ba-**lit gor**-la/ras-**tro**-yen zhi-**lu**-dak*
He has diarrhoea/ earache	**У меня понос/болит ухо** *umi-**nya** pa-**nos**/ba-**lit** y-kha*
I am constipated	**У меня запор** *umi-**nya** za-**por***
I have a pain here/ in my chest	**У меня болит здесь/в груди** *umi-**nya** ba-**lit zdyes'**/vgru-**di***
He has been stung/ bitten	**Его ужалили/покусали** *ye-**vo** u-**zha**-lili/paku-**sa**-li*
He can't breathe/ walk	**Он не может дышать/ходить** ***on** ni mo-zhit di-**schat'**/kha-**dit'***
She has a temperature	**У нее температура** *uni-**yo** timpira-**tu**-ra*

DOCTOR 2

I can't sleep/swallow	**Я не могу спать/глотать** *ya nima-gu spat'/gla-tat'*
She has been sick	**Ее вырвало** *ye-yo vir-vala*
I am diabetic/I am pregnant	**У меня диабет/Я беременна** *umi-nya dia-byet/ya bi-rye-minna*
I am allergic to penicillin/cortisone	**У меня аллергия на пенициллин/кортизон** *umi-nya alir-gi-ya na pinitsi-lin/karti-zon*
I have high blood pressure	**У меня повышенное давление** *umi-nya pa-vi-schinaye dav-lye-niye*
My blood group is A positive/negative	**У меня вторая группа крови резус положительный/отрицательный** *umi-nya fta-ra-ya gru-pa kro-vi rye-zus pala-zhi-til'nii/arti-tsa-til'nii*

THE DOCTOR MAY SAY:

Вам нужен покой *vam nu-zhin pa-koi*	You must stay in bed
Его нужно госпитализировать *ye-vo nuzh-na gospitali-zi-ravat'*	He will have to go to hospital
Вам нужна операция *vam nuzh-na api-ra-tsiya*	You will need an operation
Принимайте это три/четыре раза в день *prini-mai-tye e-ta tri/chi-ti-ri ra-za vdyen'*	Take this three/four times a day

See also **ACCIDENTS – INJURIES, EMERGENCIES**

DRINKS

Streetwise

Tea is drunk throughout the day, usually black or with lemon. Coffee is also drunk black or with condensed milk. A rather unusual drink to try in summer is **квас** (**kvas**) *made from fermented brown bread and sold from roadside tankers. Look out for cafés* **кафе** (ka-**fye**), *ice-cream parlours* **кафе-мороженое** (ka-**fye** ma-**ro**-zhinaye) *and fruit juice parlours* **соки-воды** (**so**-ki-**vo**-di) *where a wide range of flavours can be sampled.*

A coffee/tea, please	**Один кофе/чай, пожалуйста** a-*din* **ko**-fye/**chai** pa-**zha**-lusta
Two cups of tea	**Две чашки чая** *dvye* **chasch**-ki **cha**-ya
Do you have milk/lemon?	**У вас есть молоко/лимон** uvas **yest'** mala-**ko**/li-**mon**
A glass of lemonade/apple juice	**Стакан лимонада/яблочного сока** sta-**kan** lima-**na**-da/**yab**-lachnava **so**-ka
A bottle of mineral water	**Бутылку минеральной воды** bu-**til**-ku mini-**ral'**-nai va-**di**
Do you have...?	**У вас есть...?** uvas **yest'**...
With ice, please	**Со льдом, пожалуйста** sal'-**dom** pa-**zha**-lusta
Another coffee, please	**Еще один кофе, пожалуйста** i-**shcho** a-**din** **ko**-fye pa-**zha**-lusta

See also **WINES AND SPIRITS**

DRIVING

Streetwise

You should plan your route in advance and keep to Intourist-approved itineraries and pre-booked accommodation. An international driving licence is required and you must display a nationality sticker on your car. If you take your own car, a customs certificate has to be filled in, which is stamped both on arrival and departure. You will not be allowed to drive more than 500 km per day and inter-city night driving is forbidden to foreigners.

All the arrangements were made by Intourist
Все организовано Интуристом
fsyo argani-zo-vana intu-ris-tam

This is my route approved by Intourist
Это мой маршрут, одобренный Интуристом
e-ta moi mar-schrut a-dob-rinii intu-ris-tam

How many kilometres to…?
Сколько километров до…?
skol'-ka kila-myet-raf da…

When will it get dark?
Когда стемнеет?
kag-da stim-nye-it

I'd like to arrange car insurance
Я хочу застраховать машину
ya kha-chu zastrakha-vat' ma-schi-nu

The condition of my car is good/average/poor
Моя машина в хорошем/среднем/плохом состоянии
ma-ya ma-schi-na f kha-ro-schim/sryed-nim/pla-khom sasta-ya-nii

How much is this in pounds/dollars?
Сколько это в фунтах стерлингов/ в долларах?
skol'-ka e-ta ffun-takh styer-lingaf/vdo-larakh

See also ACCIDENTS – CARS, BREAKDOWNS, PETROL STATION, TRAFFIC RULES

Streetwise

Be sure to book a table in advance through the hotel Service Bureau and prepare to enjoy a traditional night out. There's often a live band and diners take to the floor between courses. Expect to spend an hour or two on the wonderful selection of hors d'œuvre **закуски** (za-**kus**-ki). *Try regional cuisine such as Armenian and Georgian and look out for the good value buffet lunches* **шведский стол** (schvye-tskii **stol**), *'Swedish table', on offer in many of the hotels.*

Can you recommend a restaurant?	**Вы можете порекомендовать ресторан?** *vi* **mo**-zhiti parikaminda-**vat'** rista-**ran**
I'd like to book a table for four, please	**Я хочу заказать столик на четверых, пожалуйста** *ya kha-**chu** zaka-**zat' sto**-lik na chitvi-**rikh** pa-**zha**-lusta*
May we see the menu, please	**Дайте, пожалуйста, меню** *dai-tye pa-**zha**-lusta mi-**nyu***
We'll take the set menu, please	**Мы будем есть комплексный обед** *mi **bu**-dim yest' **komp**-liksnii a-**byet***
We'd like a drink first	**Мы хотели бы сначала напитки** *mi kha-**tye**-li bi sna-**cha**-la na-**pit**-ki*
Could we have some more bread/water?	**Можно еще хлеба/воды?** *mozh-na i-**shcho** khlye-ba/va-**di***
We'd like a dessert/ some mineral water	**Мы хотим десерт/минеральной воды** *mi kha-**tim** di-**syert**/mini-**ral'**-nai va-**di***
The bill, please	**Счет, пожалуйста** *shchot pa-**zha**-lusta*
Is service included?	**Счет включает обслуживание?** *shchot fklyu-**cha**-it ap-**slu**-zhivaniye*

See also **DRINKS, ORDERING, PAYING**

EMERGENCIES

Streetwise

In case of emergency, notify the Intourist representative or the hotel Service Bureau as soon as possible. Emergency numbers are:
FIRE BRIGADE **01**, POLICE **02**, AMBULANCE **03**

Fire!	**Пожар!** *pa-zhar*
Call a doctor/an ambulance!	**Вызовите доктора/скорую!** *vi-zaviti dok-tara/sko-ruyu*
We must get him to hospital	**Ему нужно в больницу** *ye-mu nuzh-na vbal'-ni-tsu*
Fetch help quickly!	**Позовите на помощь, быстро!** *paza-vi-ti na po-mashch bis-tra*
Get the police!	**Вызовите милицию!** *vi-zaviti mi-li-tsiyu*
Where's the nearest hospital?	**Где ближайшая больница?** *gdye bli-zhai-schaya bal'-ni-tsa*
I've lost my credit card/wallet	**Я потерял(а) кредитную карточку/ кошелек** *ya pati-ryal(a) kri-dit-nuyu kar-tachku/kaschi-lyok*
My child is missing	**Мой ребенок потерялся** *moi ri-byo-nak pati-ryal-sya*
My passport has been stolen	**У меня украли паспорт** *umi-nya u-kra-li pas-part*
I've forgotten my ticket/my key	**Я забыл(а) билет/ключи** *ya za-bil(a) bi-lyet/klyu-chi*

See also **ACCIDENTS, BREAKDOWNS, DENTIST, DOCTOR**

Streetwise

Tickets for classical concerts, opera, ballet and folk ensembles can be obtained through the Intourist representative. Sometimes the price includes round trip transportation to your hotel. Performances usually begin between 1900 and 2000.

What ballet/opera is on today?	**Какой/какая сегодня балет/опера?** *ka-koi/ka-ka-ya si-vod-nya ba-lyet/o-pira*
Can you recommend something for the children?	**Вы можете посоветовать что-нибудь для детей?** *vi mo-zhiti pasa-vye-tavat' shchto-nibut' dlya di-tyei*
What is there to do in the evenings?	**Куда можно пойти вечером?** *ku-da mozh-na pai-ti vye-chiram*
We'd like to reserve two tickets	**Мы хотим заказать два билета** *mi kha-tim zaka-zat' dva bi-lye-ta*
How much are the tickets?	**Сколько стоят билеты?** *skol'-ka sto-yat bi-lye-ti*
When does the performance begin/end?	**Когда начало/конец представления?** *kag-da na-cha-la/ka-nyets pritstav-lye-niya*
Is there a puppet theatre on?	**Работает ли кукольный театр?** *ra-bo-tait li ku-kal'nii ti-atr*
Is there a swimming pool?	**Здесь есть бассейн?** *zdyes' yest' ba-sein*

See also **FERRIES, NIGHTLIFE, SIGHTSEEING**

FERRIES

Streetwise

You can take a short one-way or round-trip boat ride along the great Russian rivers by slow boat **корабль** *(ka-rabl') or hydrofoil* **ракета** *(ra-kye-ta [метеор (miti-or)]). Book through the Intourist representative or buy a ticket from the ticket office at the departure point.*

What time is the next sailing?	**Когда отходит следующий рейс?** *kag-da at-kho-dit slye-dushchii ryeis*
A single/return ticket to…	**Билет до/туда и обратно…** *bi-lyet da/tu-da iab-rat-na…*
How long does the trip take?	**Сколько длится прогулка?** *skol'-ka dlit-sa pra-gul-ka*
Can we eat on board?	**Можем ли мы поесть на борту?** *mo-zhim li mi pa-yest' nabar-tu*
When does the boat/ hydrofoil arrive at…?	**Когда корабль/ракета прибывает в…?** *kag-da ka-brabl'/ra-kye-ta pribi-va-it v…*
Does it stop anywhere?	**Делает ли он/она остановки?** *dye-lait li on/a-na asta-nof-ki*
Where are the toilets?	**Где туалет?** *gdye tua-lyet*
Can we go out on deck?	**Можно нам выйти на палубу?** *mozh-na nam vii-ti na pa-lubu*
Where can I have a cup of coffee/tea?	**Где можно выпить чашку кофе/чая?** *gdye mozh-na vi-pit' chasch-ku ko-fye/cha-ya*

See also SIGHTSEEING

GIFTS AND SOUVENIRS

Streetwise

Hand-painted wooden dolls, embroidery, folk art and lace are good buys as souvenirs and are available at all the foreign currency shops and many of the local shops. Traditional fur hats with ear flaps are also popular and a necessity for the winter tourist. Posters and records are good value.

Where can we buy souvenirs?	**Где можно купить сувениры?** *gdye mozh-na ku-pit' suvi-ni-ri*
Do I pay with roubles/ pounds/dollars?	**Платить в рублях/фунтах/долларах?** *pla-tit' v rub-lyakh/fun-takh/do-larakh*
I want to buy a present for my husband/wife	**Я хочу купить подарок мужу/жене** *ya kha-chu ku-pit' pa-da-rak mu-zhu/zhi-nye*
What traditional gifts do you have?	**Какие традиционные сувениры у вас есть?** *ka-ki-ye traditsi-on-nii suvi-ni-ri u vas yest'*
I would like a carrier bag	**Мне нужен (полиэтиленовый) пакет** *mnye nu-zhin (paliti-lye-navii) pa-kyet*
Is this hand-made?	**Это ручная работа?** *e-ta ruch-na-ya ra-bo-ta*
Have you anything suitable for a young child?	**У вас есть что-нибудь для маленького ребенка?** *uvas yest' schto-nibut' dlya ma-lin'kava ri-byon-ka*
I want something cheaper/more expensive	**Я хочу что-нибудь подешевле/подороже** *ya kha-chu schto-nibut' padi-schev-li/pada-ro-zhi*
Please wrap it up for me	**Заверните, пожалуйста** *zavir-ni-ti pa-zha-lusta*

See also **BUYING, PAYING, SHOPPING**

GRAMMAR 1

Russian grammar is very different to English grammar and this summary should give you a brief outline to help you use this book.

Nouns can be masculine, feminine or neuter. Noun genders are easily recognizable by their endings (except for those ending in **ь** which could be either masculine or feminine).

Endings are as follows:

m: **consonant, й, ь**	**дом, чай, день**	*dom, chai, dyen'*
f: **а, я, ь**	**книга, неделя, ночь**	*kni-ga, ni-dye-lya, noch*
nt: **о, ё, е**	**окно, бельё, море**	*ak-no, bil'-yo, mo-rye*

Plural endings are as follows:
consonant, а, я become **и, ы**:

mother **мама**	*mothers* **мамы**	*ma-ma*	*ma-mi*
baby-sitter **няня**	*baby-sitters* **няни**	*nya-nya*	*nya-ni*

о, е become **а, я**:

letter **письмо**	*letters* **письма**	*pis'-mo*	*pis'-ma*
sea **море**	*seas* **моря**	*mo-rye*	*mo-rya*

consonant becomes **ья**:

brother **брат**	*brothers* **братья**	*brat*	*bra-tya*

Russian has no definite or indefinite article, so that the word **дом** may be translated *the house* or *a house* according to the context.

Nouns, adjectives and pronouns decline in Russian, which means that their endings change according to the part they play in the sentence, i.e. subject (*the country is big* **страна большая** *stra-na bal'-scha-ya*), object (*I love the country* **я люблю страну** *ya lyu-blyu stra-nu*), or indirect object, often used with a preposition, e.g. *in, to* (*there are many people in the country* **в стране много людей** *fstra-nye mno-ga lyu-dyei*), etc. Consult a grammar for declension tables and how they apply, but you should be understood with the nominative (subject) case.

Adjectives decline and agree with the nouns they qualify in number, gender and case. The nominative (subject) adjective endings are:

m:	**ый, ий, ой**
f:	**ая, яя**
nt:	**ое, ее**

We have given both masculine and feminine endings in the Russian-English dictionary section.

Adverbs usually end in **o** and don't change. They are often formed from adjectives by changing the endings **ый, ий** to **o**, e.g. *good* **хороший** *kha-ro-schii* changes to **хорошо** *khara-scho* to form the adverb *well*.

Pronouns also decline. Personal pronouns are as follows:

I	*you*	*he*	*she*	*it*	*we*	*you*	*they*
я	**ты**	**он**	**она**	**оно**	**мы**	**вы**	**они**
ya	*ti*	*on*	*a-na*	*a-no*	*mi*	*vi*	*a-ni*

Ты is used to address children and friends: **вы** is the polite form.

Verbs

Russian has only three tenses – present, past and future. However, verbs have two aspects – the imperfective and the perfective. The imperfective is used when the action is unfinished or incomplete (*I write, I was writing, I shall be writing*), while the perfective aspect is used when the action is completed (*I wrote, I've written, I shall have written*).

Verbs change their endings according to the person and number in the present and future tenses, and according to number and gender in the past. You will notice that phrases using the past tense, e.g. *I've lost my key,* give both masculine and feminine verb endings.

Most infinitives end in **ать, ять** (1st conjugation); **ить** (2nd conjugation). The present tense of regular verbs is as follows:

GRAMMAR 3

читать – *to read* (1st conjugation)   *chi-tat'*

I read	я чита-ю	*ya chi-ta-yu*
you read	ты чита-ешь	*ti chi-ta-isch*
he/she reads	он/она чита-ет	*on/a-na chi-ta-it*
we read	мы чита-ем	*mi chi-ta-im*
you read	вы чита-ете	*vi chi-ta-itye*
they read	они чита-ют	*a-ni chi-ta-yut*

past tense:

m:	я, ты, он читал	*ya, ti, on chi-tal*
f:	я, ты, она читала	*ya, ti, a-na chi-ta-la*
m, f, pl:	мы, вы, они читали	*mi, vi, a-ni chi-ta-li*

говорить – *to speak* (2nd conjugation)   *gava-rit'*

I speak	я говор-ю	*ya gava-ryu*
you speak	ты говор-ишь	*ti gava-risch*
he/she speaks	он/она говор-ит	*on/a-na gava-rit*
we speak	мы говор-им	*mi gava-rim*
you speak	вы говор-ите	*vi gava-ri-tye*
they speak	они говор-ят	*a-ni gava-ryat*

past tense:

m:	я, ты, он говорил	*ya, ti, on gava-ril*
f:	я, ты, она говорила	*ya, ti, a-na gava-ri-la*
m, f, pl:	мы, вы, они говорили	*mi, vi, a-ni gava-ri-li*

The verb *to be* is not used in the present tense, so that **где дом?** *gdye dom* means *where is the house?*

Verbs of motion – a distinction is made in Russian between going on foot (**ходить** *kha-dit'*, **идти** *it-ti*) and going by some other form of locomotion (**ездить** *yez-dit'*, **ехать** *ye-khat'*). Be sure to use the right verb when asking for directions.

Word order is fluid in Russian. If in doubt, keep to the same order as in English.

See also **ALPHABET, PRONUNCIATION**

Streetwise

There are two forms of address: formal and informal. You should only use the informal **ты** (**ti**) when talking to someone you know well. The usual word for you (singular and plural) is **вы** (**vi**). This is the form that has been used in this book.

Hello	**Привет** pri-**vyet**
Good morning/ Good afternoon/ Good evening	**Доброе утро/Добрый день/вечер** **dob**-raye **u**-tra/ **dob**-rii **dyen'**/ **dob**-rii **vye**-chir
Goodbye	**До свидания** dasvi-**da**-niya
Good night	**Спокойной ночи** spa-**koi**-nai **no**-chi
How do you do?	**Здравствуйте!** zdrast-**vuitye**
Pleased to meet you	**Приятно познакомиться** pri-**yat**-na pazna-**ko**-mitsa
How are you?	**Как поживаете?** **kak** pazhi-**va**-yeti
Fine, thank you	**Спасибо, отлично** spa-**si**-ba at-**lich**-na
See you soon	**До скорого свидания** da **sko**-rava svi-**da**-niya
See you later	**До встречи** da **fstrye**-chi

See also **CONVERSATION**

HAIRDRESSER'S

Streetwise

Hairdressing salons can be found in most tourist hotels under the name **парикмахерская** *(parik-ma-khirskaya). A gift of quality toiletries or make-up makes a much appreciated gift.*

I'd like to make an appointment	**Я хочу записаться** *ya kha-chu zapi-sat-sa*
A cut and blow-dry, please	**Стрижку и укладку, пожалуйста** *strisch-ku i u-klat-ku pa-zha-lusta*
A shampoo and set	**Помыть и уложить** *pa-mit' i ula-zhit'*
Not too short	**Не очень коротко** *ni o-chin' ko-ratka*
Not too much off the back/fringe	**Не слишком коротко сзади/спереди** *ni slisch-kam ko-ratka zza-di/spye-ridi*
Take more off the top/the sides	**Покороче сверху/с боков** *paka-ro-chi svyer-khu/zba-kof*
My hair is permed/tinted	**У меня перманент/крашеные волосы** *umi-nya pirma-nyent/kra-schiniye vo-lasi*
My hair is naturally curly/straight	**У меня волосы вьются/прямые от природы** *umi-nya vo-lasi vyut-sa/pri-mii at pri-ro-di*
It's too hot	**Очень горячо** *o-chin' gari-cho*

Streetwise

When you check in at the hotel you exchange your passport and visa for an identity card **пропуск** (**pro**-pusk). This enables you to collect your key from the key lady **дежурная** (di-**zhur**-naya) on your floor. You may also be asked to produce the card when entering the hotel. It is also useful to show taxi drivers, as it carries the name of the hotel.

I have reserved a room in the name of…	**Я забронировал(а) комнату на имя…** ya zabra-**ni**-raval(a) **kom**-natu na **i**-mya…
Where can I park my car?	**Где можно запарковать машину?** gdye **mozh**-na zaparka-**vat'** ma-**schi**-nu
Could you have my luggage taken up?	**Вы можете поднести мой багаж?** vi **mo**-zhiti padnis-**ti** moi ba-**gasch**
What time is breakfast/dinner?	**Во сколько завтрак/ужин?** va **skol'**-ka **zaf**-trak/**u**-zhin
Could I eat earlier/ later	**Могу ли я поесть раньше/позже?** ma-**gu** li ya pa-**yest'** **ran'**-schi/**poz**-zhi
Where is the Service Bureau?	**Где Бюро Обслуживания?** gdye byu-**ro** ap-**slu**-zhivaniya
Can I have my key?	**Можно мой ключ?** **mozh**-na moi **klyuch**
We'll be back very late	**Мы вернемся очень поздно** mi vir-**nyom**-sya **o**-chin' **poz**-na
Where is the foreign currency shop?	**Где валютный магазин?** gdye va-**lyut**-nii maga-**zin**
I shall be leaving tomorrow morning	**Я уезжаю завтра утром** ya uye-**zha**-yu **zaf**-tra **u**-tram

See also **ACCOMMODATION, ROOM SERVICE, PAYING**

LUGGAGE

Where do I check in my luggage?
Где регистрация багажа?
*gdye rigis-**tra**-tsiya baga-**zha***

Where is the luggage from the London flight?
Где выдача багажа из Лондона?
*gdye **vi**-dacha baga-**zha** iz **lon**-dana*

Our luggage has not arrived
Наш багаж не прибыл
*nasch ba-**gasch** ni **pri**-bil*

My suitcase was damaged in transit
Мой чемодан повредили при перевозке
*moi chima-**dan** pavri-**di**-li pri piri-**vos**-kye*

Where is the left-luggage office?
Где камера хранения?
*gdye **ka**-mira khra-**nye**-niya*

Is there a porter?
Здесь есть носильщик?
*zdyes' **yest'** na-**sil'**-shchik*

It's very heavy
Это очень тяжело
*e-ta **o**-chin' tizhi-**lo***

Can you help me with my bags, please?
Помогите мне с вещами, пожалуйста
*pama-**gi**-ti mnye svi-**shcha**-mi pa-**zha**-lusta*

Take my bag to a taxi
Поднесите мою сумку к такси
*padni-**si**-tye ma-**yu** sum-ku ktak-**si***

I can manage this one myself
Я справлюсь с этим сам(сама)
*ya **sprav**-lyus' **se**-tim **sam**(sa-**ma**)*

I sent my luggage on in advance
Я отправил(а) багаж заранее
*ya at-**pra**-vil(a) ba-**gasch** za-**ra**-niye*

MAPS AND GUIDES

Streetwise

Maps and guides are available from the hotel bookstalls and foreign
currency shops. It is well worth spending some time learning the
Cyrillic alphabet before you arrive so that you can recognize street
names and signs.

Where is the nearest
newsstand?

Где ближайший газетный киоск?
gdye bli-zhai-schii ga-zyet-nii ki-osk

I want a street map
of the city

Мне нужна карта города
mnye nuzh-na kar-ta go-rada

I need a road map
of...

Мне нужен атлас дорог...
mnye nu-zhin at-las da-rok...

Where can I buy an
English newspaper?

**Где я могу купить газеты на
английском языке?**
*gdye ya ma-gu ku-pit' ga-zye-ti naan-glis-kam
yazi-kye*

Can you show me
on the map?

Можете показать мне по карте?
mo-zhiti paka-zat' mnye pa kar-tye

Do you have a
guidebook in English?

**У вас есть путеводитель на английском
языке?**
uvas yest' putiva-di-tyel' naan-glis-kam

Do you have a
guidebook to the
museum?

У вас есть путеводитель по музею?
uvas yest' putiva-di-tyel' pa mu-zye-yu

I need an English–
Russian dictionary

Мне нужен англо-русский словарь
mnye nu-zhin an-gla-rus-kii sla-var'

See also **DIRECTIONS**

MEASUREMENTS

a litre of...
литр...
litr...

a kilo of...
кило...
ki-lo...

a pound of...
фунт...
funt...

100 grams of...
сто грамм...
sto gram...

half a kilo of...
полкило...
polki-lo...

a half bottle of...
поллитра...
pol-li-tra...

a slice of...
кусок...
ku-sok...

a portion of...
порция...
por-tsiya...

a dozen...
дюжина...
dyu-zhina...

10 roubles worth of...
на десять рублей...
na dye-sit' rub-lyei...

a third
треть
tryet'

two thirds
две трети
dvye trye-ti

a quarter
четверть
chyet-virt'

three quarters
три четверти
tri chyet-virti

ten per cent
десять процентов
dye-sit' pra-tsen-taf

more...
больше...
bol'-schi...

less...
меньше...
myen'-schi...

enough...
достаточно...
das-ta-tachna...

twice
в два раза
vdva ra-za

three times
в три раза
ftri ra-za

See also **CONVERSION CHARTS, NUMBERS**

MENUS

The Russians eat three main meals a day:

Breakfast – завтрак (*zaf*-trak) usually consists of fruit juice, brown and white bread, rolls, preserves and cheese or cold meats. The hot dish might be porridge **каша** (*ka*-sha), cheese cakes **сырники** (*sir*-niki) served with soured cream or an egg dish such as omelette. Tea and coffee are normally drunk black.

Lunch – обед (*a*-**byet**) is the main meal eaten between 1300 and 1400. It consists of hors d'œuvre **закуски** (*za*-**kus**-ki) followed by a 'first course' of home-made soup. The main dish is usually meat, chicken or fish served with a garnish of vegetables or rice. Dessert might consist of cake or delicious rich ice cream served with tea or coffee.

Dinner – ужин (*u*-zhin) is similar to lunch but does not include soup. For a true flavour of Russian cuisine, attend a Gala dinner and enjoy a staggering array of *za*-**kus**-ki. Don't forget the vodka toasts – drunk neat and all in one – and remember to follow it up with a soft drink or some bread!

Menus are often very long, but usually only the dishes marked with prices are available.

May we see the menu, please	**Дайте, пожалуйста, меню** *dai*-tye pa-**zha**-lusta mi-**nyu**
Is there a local speciality?	**У вас есть фирменное блюдо?** *uvas* **yest'** *fir*-minaye **blyu**-da
What is in this dish?	**Из чего приготовлено это блюдо?** *is chi*-**vo** priga-**tov**-lina *e*-ta **blyu**-da

See also **EATING OUT, ORDERING, PAYING**

MONEY

Streetwise

The present currency is the rouble which is divided into 100 kopeks. Banks offer a favourable rate of exchange and can be found at the airports and in hotels. Remember to present your customs declaration form. Be wary of black marketeers who may try offering you large denomination banknotes which have been withdrawn from circulation.

I haven't enough money	**У меня не хватает денег** *umi-**nya** ni khva-**ta**-it **dye**-nyek*
Have you any change?	**У вас есть сдача?** *uvas **yest'** **zda**-cha*
Can you change a 100 rouble note?	**Вы можете разменять сто рублей?** *vi **mo**-zhiti razmi-**nyat' sto** rub-**lyei***
I'd like to change these traveller's cheques	**Я хочу обменять дорожные чеки** *ya kha-**chu** abmi-nyat' da-**rozh**-nii **chye**-ki*
Where can I change some money?	**Где можно обменять деньги?** *gdye **mozh**-na abmi-**nyat' dyen'**-gi*
What is the rate for sterling/dollars?	**Какой курс фунта/доллара?** *ka-**koi** kurs **fun**-ta/**do**-lara*
Here is my customs declaration form	**Вот моя декларация** *vot ma-**ya** dikla-**ra**-tsiya*
Can I get a cash advance with my credit card?	**Могу ли я получить деньги по кредитной карточке?** *ma-**gu** li ya palu-**chit' dyen'**-gi pa kri-**dit**-nai **kar**-tachkye*

See also **NUMBERS, PAYING**

Streetwise

Restaurants **ресторан** *(rista-ran) often have live music and dancing. Intourist hotels have a bar offering local and imported drinks which must be paid for with foreign currency, and several hotels now have casinos.*

What is there to do in the evenings?	**Куда здесь можно пойти вечером?** *ku-da zdes' mozh-na pai-ti vye-chiram*
Where can we go dancing?	**Где можно потанцевать?** *gdye mozh-na patantsi-vat'*
Are there any good concerts on?	**Есть ли сейчас хорошие концерты?** *yest' li si-chas kha-ro-schii kan-tser-ti*
How do we get to the concert/casino?	**Как нам добраться на концерт/в казино?** *kak nam da-brat-sa nakan-tsert/fkazi-no*
How much does it cost to get in?	**Сколько стоит вход?** *skol'-ka sto-it fkhot*
We'd like to reserve two seats for tonight	**Мы хотели бы заказать два билета на вечер** *mi kha-tye-li bi zaka-zat' dva bi-lye-ta na vye-chir*
Is there a bar/a restaurant?	**Там есть бар/ресторан?** *tam yest' bar/rista-ran*
What time does the performance begin?	**Во сколько начинается представление?** *va skol'-ka nachi-na-itsa pritstav-lye-niye*
Can we get there by Metro/bus?	**Можно ли туда доехать на метро/автобусе?** *mozh-na li tu-da da-ye-khat' nami-tro/af-to-busi*

See also **EATING OUT, ENTERTAINMENT**

NUMBERS

0	ноль *nol'*	11	одиннадцать a-**di**-natsat'	30	тридцать *tri*-tsat'
1	один a-**din**	12	двенадцать dvi-**na**-tsat'	40	сорок **so**-rak
2	два *dva*	13	тринадцать tri-**na**-tsat'	50	пятьдесят pidi-**syat**
3	три *tri*	14	четырнадца chi-**tir**-natsat'	60	шестьдесят schizdi-**syat**
4	четыре chi-**ti**-ri	15	пятнадцать pit-**na**-tsat'	70	семьдесят **syem**-disyet
5	пять *pyat'*	16	шестнадцать schis-**na**-tsat'	80	восемьдесят **vo**-simdisyet
6	шесть *schest'*	17	семнадцать sim-**na**-tsat'	90	девяносто divi-**no**-sta
7	семь *syem'*	18	восемнадцать vasim-**na**-tsat'	100	сто *sto*
8	восемь **vo**-sim'	19	девятнадцать divit-**na**-tsat'	200	двести **dvye**-sti
9	девять **dye**-vit'	20	двадцать **dva**-tsat'	1000	тысяча **ti**-sicha
10	десять **dye**-sit'	21	двадцать один **dva**-tsat' a-**din**	1,000,000	миллион mili- **on**

1st	первый **pyer**-vii	5th	пятый **pya**-tii	9th	девятый di-**vya**-tii
2nd	второй fta-**roi**	6th	шестой schis-**toi**	10th	десятый di-**sya**-tii
3rd	третий **trye**-tii	7th	седьмой sid'-**moi**		
4th	четвёрый chit-**vyor**-tii	8th	восьмой vas'-**moi**		

ORDERING

Streetwise

The hotel Service Bureau can book a table in advance. Ask their advice on restaurants and regional cuisine and learn the names of dishes you would like to try. Menus run into several pages, but only dishes marked with a price are usually available.

Do you have a set menu?	**У вас есть комплексное меню?** uvas **yest'** **komp**-liksnaye mi-**nyu**
May we see the wine list?	**Можно посмотреть список вин?** **mozh**-na pasmat-**ryet' spi**-sak **vin**
What do you recommend?	**Что вы порекомендуете?** **schto** vi parikamyen-**du**-iti
Is there a local speciality?	**У вас есть фирменное блюдо?** uvas **yest' fir**-minaye **blyu**-da
Do you have soup?	**У вас есть суп?** uvas **yest' sup**
What is in this dish?	**Из чего приготовлено это блюдо?** is chi-**vo** priga-**tov**-lina e-ta **blyu**-da
Is it served with vegetables?	**Это подается с овощами?** e-ta pada-**yot**-sa sava-**shcha**-mi
Rare/medium/well done, please	**С кровью/средне/зажаренный, пожалуйста** skrov-yu/**sryed**-nye/za-**zha**-rinii pa-**zha**-lusta
We'd like a dessert/ some coffee, please	**Принесите, пожалуйста, десерт/кофе** prini-**si**-tye pa-**zha**-lusta di-**syert**/**ko**-fye

See also **COMPLAINTS, EATING OUT, PAYING, WINES AND SPIRITS**   55

PAYING

Streetwise

Credit cards are accepted in foreign currency shops and foreign currency restaurants. Traveller's cheques can be exchanged for roubles, but Eurocheques are not currently accepted.

Can I have the bill, please?	**Принесите счет, пожалуйста** *prini-**si**-tye **shchot** pa-**zha**-lusta*
Is service/tax included?	**Обслуживание/налог включено в счет?** *ap-**slu**-zhivaniye/na-**lok** fklyuchi-**no** fschot*
What does that come to?	**Итого, сколько всего?** *ita-**vo skol'**-ka fsi-**vo***
How much is that?	**Сколько это стоит?** ***skol'**-ka **e**-ta **sto**-it*
Can I pay with roubles?	**Могу ли я заплатить в рублях?** *ma-**gu** li **ya** zapla-**tit'** vrub-**lyakh***
Can I pay by credit card?	**Вы принимаете кредитные карточки?** *vi prini-**ma**-iti kri-**dit**-nii **kar**-tachki*
Do you accept roubles or currency?	**Вы принимаете рубли или валюту?** *vi prini-**ma**-iti rub-**li** ili va-**lyu**-tu*
I think you've given me the wrong change	**Мне кажется, вы дали мне сдачу неверно** *mnye **ka**-zhitsa vi **da**-li mnye **zda**-chu ni-**vyer**-na*
I'd like a receipt, please	**Дайте мне чек, пожалуйста** ***dai**-ti mnye **chyek** pa-**zha**-lusta*

See also **BUYING, MONEY**

| My name is… | **Меня зовут…** |
| | mi-**nya** za-**vut** … |

| My date of birth is… | **Я родился(родилась)…** |
| | ya ra-**dil**-sya(radi-**las'**)… |

| My address is… | **Мой адрес…** |
| | moi **a**-driz… |

| I come from Britain/America | **Я приехал(а) из Великобритании/Америки** |
| | ya pri-**ye**-khal(a) iz vilikabri-**ta**-nii/a-**mye**-riki |

| I live in… | **Я живу в…** |
| | ya zhi-**vu** v… |

| My passport/driving licence number is… | **Номер моего паспорта/водительских прав…** |
| | **no**-mir mai-**vo pas**-parta/va-**di**-til'skikh **praf**… |

| My blood group is… | **Моя группа крови…** |
| | ma-**ya gru**-pa **kro**-vi… |

| I work in an office/a factory | **Я работаю в конторе/на фабрике** |
| | ya ra-**bo**-tayu fkan-**to**-ri/na **fab**-rikye |

| I am a secretary/manager | **Я секретарь/менеджер** |
| | ya sikri-**tar'**/**me**-nedzher |

| I'm here on holiday/business | **Здесь я отдыхаю/работаю** |
| | **zdyes'** ya atdi-**kha**-yu/ra-**bo**-tayu |

| There are four of us | **Мы здесь вчетвером** |
| | **mi** zdyes' fchitvi-**rom** |

| My daughter is six | **Моей дочери шесть лет** |
| | ma-**yei do**-chiri **schest' lyet'** |

PETROL STATION

Streetwise

Petrol is sold according to grade. Be sure to get 90+ octane or your car will barely leave the pump. Unleaded petrol is currently impossible to find. Petrol is paid for in advance using coupons purchased for foreign currency at the borders (although you may find some garages will accept roubles).

20 litres of 93 octane	**Двадцать литров девяносто третьего бензина** *dva-tsat' li-traf divi-nos-ta trye-tyeva bin-zi-na*
Do you take coupons or cash?	**Вы отпускаете по талонам или за деньги?** *vi atpus-ka-iti pata-lo-nam i-li za dyen'-gi*
Fill it up, please	**Заполните до верха, пожалуйста** *za-pol-nitye da vyer-kha pa-zha-lusta*
Do you have oil/water?	**У вас есть масло/вода?** *uvas yest' ma-sla/va-da*
The tyres need more air	**Шины нужно подкачать** *schi-ni nuzh-na patka-chat'*
Where can I wash the car?	**Где можно помыть машину?** *gdye mozh-na pa-mit' ma-schi-nu*
Please fill my can with petrol/oil	**Налейте в канистру бензин/масло, пожалуйста** *na-lyei-ti fka-nis-tru bin-zin/ma-sla pa-zha-lusta*
Is there a telephone/a lavatory?	**Здесь есть телефон/туалет?** *zdyes' yest' tili-fon/tua-lyet*
How far is the next petrol station?	**Как далеко следующая бензоколонка?** *kak dali-ko slye-dushchiya binzaka-lon-ka*

See also **DRIVING ABROAD**, **PAYING**

Streetwise

Although now available in foreign currency shops, it would be wise to take a good stock of film and batteries with you and then wait till you get home to have your pictures developed. If you want to photograph people, you should ask their permission.

I need a colour/black and white film	**Мне нужна цветная/черно-белая пленка** *mnye nuzh-**na** tsvit-**na**-ya/**chor**-na-**bye**-laya **plyon**-ka*
It is for prints/slides	**Это для фотографий/слайдов** *e-ta dlya fata-**gra**-fii/**slai**-daf*
There's something wrong with my camera	**Что-то случилось с моей камерой** *schto-ta slu-**chi**-las' sma-**yei ka**-mirai*
The film/shutter has jammed	**Пленку/затвор заело** *plyon-ku/za-**tvor** za-**ye**-la*
The rewind mechanism does not work	**Перемотка не работает** *piri-**mot**-ka ni ra-**bo**-tait*
Can you develop this film, please?	**Проявите, пожалуйста, эту пленку** *prai-**vi**-ti pa-**zha**-lusta e-tu **plyon**-ku*
When will the photos be ready?	**Когда будут готовы фотографии?** *kag-**da bu**-dut ga-**to**-vi fata-**gra**-fii*
Do you mind if I take your picture?	**Можно я вас сфотографирую?** ***mozh**-na ya **vas** sfatagra-**fi**-ruyu*
Can I take photos in here?	**Здесь можно фотографировать?** *zdyes' **mozh**-na fatagra-**fi**-ravat'*

POLICE

Streetwise

Look out for the following sign **милиция** *(mi-li-tsiya). Uniforms are grey. The emergency number is* **02**.

We should call the police	**Мы должны вызвать милицию** **mi** dalzh-**ni** **vi**-zvat' mi-**li**-tsiyu
Where is the police station?	**Где отделение милиции?** **gdye** atdi-**lye**-niye mi-**li**-tsii
My car has been broken into	**Мою машину взломали** ma-**yu** ma-**schi**-nu vzla-**ma**-li
I've been robbed	**Меня обокрали** mi-**nya** aba-**kra**-li
I have had an accident	**У меня случилась авария** umi-**nya** slu-**chi**-las' a-**va**-riya
How much is the fine?	**Сколько штраф?** **skol**'-ka **schtraf**
Can I pay at the police station?	**Могу я заплатить в отделении?** ma-**gu** ya zapla-**tit'** vatdi-**lye**-nii
I don't have my driving licence on me	**У меня нет с собой водительских прав** umi-**nya** nyet ssa-**boi** va-**di**-til'skikh **praf**
I'm very sorry, officer	**Извините, начальник** izvi-**ni**-ti na-**chal**'-nik
I didn't know the regulations	**Я не знал(а) правил** ya ni **znal**(a) **pra**-vil

See also **ACCIDENTS, CUSTOMS AND PASSPORTS, EMERGENCIES**

POST OFFICE

Streetwise

All Intourist hotels have a post office selling postcards and stamps. These can also be bought in the foreign currency shops. This avoids long queues in the Post Office **почта** (**poch**-ta).

How much is a letter to England/America?	**Сколько стоит послать письмо в Англию/Америку?** *skol'-ka **sto**-it pa-**slat'** pis'-**mo** van-gliyu/ va-**mye**-riku*
I'd like six stamps for postcards to Great Britain, please	**Шесть марок на открытки в Англию, пожалуйста** *schest' **ma**-rak naat-**krit**-ki **van**-gliyu pa-**zha**-lusta*
Where can I post this?	**Где можно это отослать?** *gdye **mozh**-na **e**-ta ata-**slat'***
I want to send a telegram to…	**Я хочу послать телеграмму в…** *ya kha-**chu** pa-**slat'** tili-**gra**-mu v…*
When will it arrive?	**Когда она дойдет?** *kag-**da** a-**na** dai-**dyot***
How much will it cost?	**Сколько это будет стоить?** *skol'-ka **e**-ta **bu**-dit **sto**-it'*
Do I have to fill in a form?	**Нужно ли мне заполнить бланк?** *nuzh-na li mnye za-**pol**-nit' blank*
I want to send this parcel	**Я хочу отослать эту посылку** *ya kha-**chu** ata-**slat'** **e**-tu pa-**sil**-ku*

PROBLEMS

Streetwise

The Intourist representative is always on hand to deal with problems.

Can you help me, please?	**Помогите мне, пожалуйста** *pama-**gi**-ti **mnye** pa-**zha**-lusta*
What is the matter?	**Что случилось?** *schto slu-**chi**-las'*
I am in trouble	**Я в затруднении** *ya vzatrud-**nye**-nii*
I don't understand	**Я не понимаю** *ya ni pani-**ma**-yu*
Do you speak English?	**Вы говорите по-английски?** *vi gava-**ri**-ti paan-**glis**-ki*
I have run out of money	**У меня кончились деньги** *umi-**nya kon'**-chilis **dyen'**-gi*
My son is lost	**Мой сын потерялся** *moi **sin** pati-**ryal**-sya*
I have lost my way	**Я заблудился(заблудилась)** *ya zablu-**dil**-sya(zablu-**di**-las')*
I have forgotten my passport	**Я забыл(а) паспорт** *ya za-**bil**(a) **pas**-part*
Please give me my passport back	**Отдайте мой паспорт, пожалуйста** *at-**dai**-ti moi **pas**-part pa-**zha**-lusta*
Where is the British Consulate?	**Где английское Консульство?** *gdye an-**glis**-kaye **kon**-sul'stva*

See also **ACCIDENTS, COMPLAINTS, EMERGENCIES, POLICE**

PRONUNCIATION

Each Russian word contains one stressed syllable and we have indicated the stressed syllable with heavy italics in the pronunciation of the Russian phrases.

The effect of this stress is to weaken the other vowels, particularly **o** and **a**. When stressed they're pronounced as written, e.g.

| **молоко** | mala-**ko** | milk | **нога** | na-**ga** | leg |

Note how all the unstressed **o**s and **a**s sound like *a* in *aloud*. The further away the vowels **и** and **e** are from the stressed syllable, the more they sound like *er* in *further*, e.g.

| **развлечение** | razvli-**chye**-niye | entertainment |

Vowels	a	e	i	o	u
Russian (hard)	**а**	**э**	**ы**	**о**	**у**
Russian (soft)	**я**	**е**	**и**	**ё**	**ю**

When the soft vowels are combined with a consonant (e.g. **p п л б д т**), that consonant becomes softened – as though a *y* had been added to the vowel:

да	pronounced	*da (d+a)*	**ло**	pronounced	*lo (l+o)*
дя	pronounced	*dya (d+ya)*	**лё**	pronounced	*lyo (l+yo)*
пэ	pronounced	*pe (p+e)*	**бу**	pronounced	*bu (b+u)*
пе	pronounced	*pye (p+ye)*	**бю**	pronounced	*byu (b+yu)*

A softened, or palatized, consonant is followed by **ь** in Russian, and we've marked this in the pronunciation with an apostrophe, e.g. **работать** ra-**bo**-tat' (to work). Be sure to press your tongue fully against the back of your upper teeth to get the right sound!

Voiced consonants **б в д з ж г** become their voiceless counter-parts **п ф т с ш к** before voiced consonants and at the end of a word, e.g.

| **друг** | **druk** | boyfriend | **завтра** | **zaf**-tra | tomorrow |

Native speakers would naturally be aware of these changes and we have reflected them in the pronunciation. To get a feel of the language, try and listen to a Russian language tape before departure.

See also **ALPHABET, GRAMMAR**

RAILWAY STATION

Streetwise

Inter-city travel is normally booked in advance through Intourist. The longest railway line in the world runs between Moscow and Vladivostock (9,300 km) with trains departing daily from Moscow at 1400.

What time are the trains to…?	**Во сколько отходят поезда на…?** *va **skol'**-ka at-**kho**-dyat paiz-**da** na…*
When is the next train to…?	**Когда будет следующий поезд на…?** *kag-**da** bu-dit **slye**-dushchii po-ist na…*
What time does it arrive?	**Во сколько он прибывает?** *va **skol'**-ka on pribi-**va**-it*
Do I have to change?	**Мне нужно делать пересадку?** *mnye **nuzh**-na **dye**-lat' piri-**sat**-ku*
A single/return to…	**В один конец/туда и обратно до…** *va-**din** ka-**nyets**/tu-**da** i ab-**rat**-na da…*
Which platform for the train to…?	**С какой платформы отходит поезд на…?** *ska-**koi** plat-**for**-mi at-**kho**-dit po-ist na…*
Where can I have a cup of coffee/tea?	**Где можно выпить чашку кофе/чая?** *gdye mozh-na vi-pit' **chasch**-ku ko-**fye**/**cha**-ya*

64

See also **LUGGAGE, TRAIN TRAVEL**

Streetwise

The vital word to know is **ремонт** *(ri-mont), meaning repair. Ask your hotel floor attendant for help.*

I have broken a glass/ the window	**Я разбил(а) стакан/окно** *ya raz-bil(a) sta-kan/a-kno*
There is a hole in my shoe/these trousers	**В этих туфлях/брюках дыра** *ve-tikh tuf-lyakh/bryu-kakh di-ra*
This is broken/torn	**Это сломано/порвано** *e-ta slo-mana/por-vana*
Can you repair this?	**Вы можете это починить?** *vi mo-zhiti e-ta pachi-nit'*
Can you do it quickly?	**Вы можете сделать это быстро?** *vi mo-zhiti zdye-lat' e-ta bis-tra*
When can you get it done by?	**Когда вы это сделаете?** *kag-da vi e-ta zdye-laiti*
I need some adhesive tape/a safety pin	**Мне нужна клейкая лента/булавка** *mnye nuzh-na klyei-kaya lyen-ta/bu-laf-ka*
The stitching has come undone	**Разошелся шов** *raza-schol-sya schof*
Where can I reheel these shoes?	**Где мне починить каблук?** *gdye mnye pachi-nit' ka-bluk*
The handle has come off	**Ручка отвалилась** *ruch-ka atva-li-las'*

See also **ACCIDENTS, BREAKDOWNS, EMERGENCIES**

ROAD CONDITIONS

Streetwise

Beware of potholes and tram tracks which are particularly hazardous in winter. Inter-city night driving is forbidden to foreigners. Don't be alarmed to find in cities that drivers use only their sidelights at night.

Is there a route that avoids the traffic?	**Есть ли путь в объезд движения?** *yest' li put' vab-yest dvi-zhe-niya*
Is the traffic heavy in the centre?	**Большое ли движение в центре?** *bal'-scho-ye li dvi-zhe-niye ftsen-tri*
What is causing this hold-up?	**Что вызвало пробку?** *schto vi-zvala prop-ku*
When will the road be clear?	**Когда дорога освободится?** *kag-da da-ro-ga asvaba-dit-sa*
Is there a detour?	**Есть ли объезд?** *yest' li ab-yest*
Is the road to… snowed up?	**Дорога на… занесена?** *da-ro-ga na… zanisi-na*
Is the pass/tunnel open?	**Открыт ли проезд/тоннель?** *at-krit li pra-yest/ta-nel'*
Do I need chains?	**Мне нужны цепи?** *mnye nuzh-ni tse-pi*
Please can you help?	**Помогите, пожалуйста** *pama-gi-ti pa-zha-lusta*

See also **DRIVING, WEATHER**

Streetwise

Room service is not customary, but most hotels have a floor attendant **дежурная** (di-**zhur**-naya) *on duty around the clock. She holds the room keys. Often a mine of useful information, she will also make tea, arrange wake-up calls and book taxis. A western trinket is a good way of showing appreciation. There is normally a coffee shop on one or more of the floors.*

Come in!	**Войдите!** vai-**di**-ti
Please call me at 7am	**Позвоните мне в семь утра, пожалуйста** pazva-**ni**-ti mnye fsyem' u-**tra** pa-**zha**-lusta
Please order a taxi for 7pm	**Закажите, пожалуйста, такси на семь вечера** zaka-**zhi**-ti pa-**zha**-lusta tak-**si** na syem' **vye**-chira
I have lost my key	**Я потерял(а) ключ** ya pati-**ryal**(a) klyuch
I have locked myself out of my room	**Я нечаянно захлопнул(а) дверь** ya ni-**cha**-ina za-**khlop**-nul(a) dvyer'
Where is the socket for my electric razor?	**Где розетка для электробритв?** gdye ra-**zyet**-ka dlya ilyektra-**britf**
I need a hairdryer/ an iron	**Мне нужен фен/утюг** mnye **nu**-zhin fyen/u-tyuk
May I have an extra blanket/pillow?	**Можно мне еще одно одеяло/одну подушку?** mozh-na mnye i-**shcho** ad-**no** adi-**ya**-la/ad-**nu** pa-**dusch**-ku
The TV/radio does not work	**Телевизор/радио не работает** tili-**vi**-zar/**ra**-dio ni ra-**bo**-tait

See also **CLEANING, COMPLAINTS, HOTEL DESK, TELEPHONE**

SHOPPING

Streetwise

Shops are normally open 0900–1300 and 1400–1900 Mon.–Sat. Department stores stay open all day. Smaller shops are identified by a sign indicating the product they sell. Markets provide a colourful selection of food produce at considerably higher prices (although still reasonable to foreigners). Beware of pickpockets in crowded places.

Where are the main shops?	**Где универмаги?** *gdye univir-**ma**-gi*
What time do the shops close?	**Во сколько закрываются магазины?** *va **skol'**-ka zakri-**va**-yutsa maga-**zi**-ni*
How much does that cost?	**Сколько это стоит?** ***skol'**-ka **e**-ta **sto**-it*
How much is it per kilo/per metre?	**Почем кило/метр?** *pa-**chyom** ki-**lo**/**myetr***
Can I try it on?	**Можно мне это примерить?** ***mozh**-na mnye **e**-ta pri-**mye**-rit'*
Where can I buy posters/records?	**Где продаются плакаты/пластинки?** *gdye prada-**yut**-sa pla-**ka**-ti/plas-**tin**-ki*
I'm looking for a gift for my wife	**Я ищу подарок жене** *ya i-**shchu** pa-**da**-rak zhi-**nye***
I'm just looking	**Я просто смотрю** *ya **pros**-ta sma-**tryu***
Have you anything suitable for a small boy?	**У вас есть что-нибудь для маленького мальчика?** *uvas **yest' shto**-nibut' dlya **ma**-lin'kava **mal'**-chika*

68

See also BUYING, GIFTS AND SOUVENIRS, PAYING

Streetwise

There are many excellent museums and entry fees are modest. Check opening hours with the hotel Service Bureau. All public buildings have huge cloakrooms for you to leave your coat: it is considered bad manners to enter anywhere with your coat on. Intourist operates a wide variety of interesting tours with the added advantage of being picked up and set down at your hotel.

What is there to see here?	**Что здесь стоит посмотреть?** *schto zdyes' **sto**-it pasma-**tryet'***
Excuse me, how do I get to…?	**Извините, как мне добраться до…?** *izvi-**ni**-ti **kak** mnye da-**brat**-sa da…*
Where is Red Square/ the museum?	**Где Красная Площадь/музей?** *gdye kras-naya **plo**-shchat'/mu-**zyei***
Where is the ticket office?	**Где билетная касса?** *gdye bi-**lyet**-naya **ka**-sa*
What time does the guided tour begin?	**Во сколько начинается экскурсия?** *va **skol'**-ka nachi-**na**-itsa iks-**kur**-siya*
How much does it cost to get in?	**Какая там входная плата?** *ka-**ka**-ya tam fkhad-**na**-ya **pla**-ta*
Can we take photographs in here?	**Здесь можно фотографировать?** *zdyes' **mozh**-na fatagra-**fi**-ravat'*
Where can I buy postcards/ ice cream?	**Где можно купить открытки/ мороженое?** *gdye **mozh**-na ku-**pit'** at-**krit**-ki/ma-**ro**-zhinaye*

See also **FERRIES, MAPS AND GUIDES, TRIPS AND EXCURSIONS**

SMOKING

Streetwise

Smoking is forbidden in many public places. The sign for No Smoking *is* **не курить!** *Western brands are available from hotel bars and at the foreign currency shops. A packet of foreign cigarettes is a good way of tipping.*

Do you mind if I smoke?	**Вы не возражаете, если я закурю?** *vi ni vazra-zha-iti yes-li ya zaku-ryu*
May I have an ashtray?	**Можно пепельницу?** *mozh-na pye-pil'nitsu*
Is this a no-smoking area?	**Здесь не курят?** *zdyes' ni ku-ryat*
A packet of..., please	**Пачку..., пожалуйста** *pach-ku..., pa-zha-lusta*
Have you got any American/British cigarettes?	**У вас есть американские/английские сигареты?** *uvas yest' amiri-kans-kii/an-glis-kii siga-rye-ti*
I'd like some pipe tobacco	**Мне нужен трубочный табак** *mnye nu-zhin tru-bachnii ta-bak*
Do you have any matches/cigars?	**У вас есть спички/сигары?** *uvas yest' spich-ki/si-ga-ri*
Can you refill my lighter?	**Вы можете зарядить мою зажигалку?** *vi mo-zhiti zari-dit' ma-yu zazhi-gal-ku*
Have you got a light?	**Огонька не найдется?** *agan'-ka ni nai-dyot-sa*

Streetwise

Some of the finest sports facilities can be found in Moscow. Try the heated open-air swimming pools where you can swim all year round, or take the Intourist sports tour which allows you access to impressive sights.

Which sports activities are available here?	**Каким спортом здесь можно заниматься?** ka-**kim** spor-tam zdyes' **mozh**-na zani-**mat**-sa
Is it possible to go fishing/riding?	**Здесь можно порыбачить/покататься верхом?** zdyes' **mozh**-na pari-**ba**-chit'/paka-**tat**-sa vir-**khom**
Where can we play tennis/golf?	**Где можно играть в теннис/гольф?** gdye **mozh**-na i-**grat**' v **te**-nis/**gol**'f
Are there any interesting walks nearby?	**Здесь есть красивые места для прогулок?** zdyes' **yest**' kra-**si**-vii mis-**ta** dlya pra-**gu**-lak
Can we rent the equipment?	**Можно взять оборудование напрокат?** **mozh**-na **vzyat**' aba-**ru**-davaniye napra-**kat**
How much does it cost per hour?	**Какая цена за час?** ka-**ka**-ya tsi-**na** za **chas**
Is there a swimming pool/sauna?	**Здесь есть бассейн/сауна?** zdyes' **yest**' ba-**sein**/**sa**-una
Where do we buy our tickets?	**Где нам купить билеты?** **gdye** nam ku-**pit**' bi-**lye**-ti
Can we take lessons?	**Мы можем брать уроки?** mi **mo**-zhim **brat**' u-**ro**-ki

See also **BEACH, TRIPS AND EXCURSIONS, WINTER SPORTS**

TAXIS

Streetwise

*Official taxis can be easily recognized from the yellow and check design on the door and the green light on the windscreen. They can be hailed or picked up at taxi ranks (**T**). It is also quite normal to hail private passing cars.*

Can you order me a taxi, please?
Вызовите мне такси, пожалуйста
vi-zaviti mnye ta-ksi pa-zha-lusta

To the main station/airport, please
На вокзал/в аэропорт, пожалуйста
na vak-zal/vaera-port pa-zha-lusta

Take me to this address
Отвезите меня по этому адресу
atvi-zi-ti mi-nya pa e-tamu a-drisu

How much will it cost?
Сколько это будет стоить?
skol'-ka e-ta bu-dit sto-it'

I'm in a hurry
Я очень спешу
ya o-chin' spi-schu

Can you wait here for a few minutes?
Вы можете подождать здесь несколько минут?
vi mo-zhiti pada-zhdat' zdyes' nyes-kal'ka mi-nut

Turn left/right here
Поверните здесь налево/направо
pavir-ni-ti zdyes' na-lye-va/na-pra-va

How much is it?
Сколько?
skol'-ka

It's more than on the meter
Это больше, чем на счетчике
e-ta bol'-schi chyem na shcho-chiki

Keep the change
Оставьте сдачу себе
a-staf-ti zda-chu si-bye

Streetwise

Local calls are free from hotels. You can book international calls at the hotel Service Bureau and take them in your room. A few hotels have phone booths where you can make direct international calls using a phone card. Enquire at the hotel Service Bureau.

I want to make an international phone call	**Я хочу позвонить за границу** *ya kha-chu pazva-nit' zagra-ni-tsu*
Can I have a line to…?	**Могу ли я позвонить в…?** *ma-gu li ya pazva-nit' v…*
The number is…	**Номер…** *no-mir…*
I want to reverse the charges	**Я хочу позвонить за счет абонента** *ya kha-chu pazva-nit' za schot aba-nyen-ta*
Have you got change for the phone?	**У вас есть монеты для телефона?** *uvas yest' ma-nye-ti dlya tili-fo-na*
What coins do I need?	**Какие мне нужны монеты?** *ka-ki-i mnye nuzh-ni ma-nye-ti*
How much is it to phone Britain/the USA?	**Сколько стоит позвонить в Англию/ Штаты?** *skol'-ka sto-it pazva-nit van-gliyu/fschta-ti*
I can't get through	**Я не могу дозвониться** *ya nima-gu dazva-ni-tsa*
The line's engaged	**Линия занята** *li-niya za-nita*

TELEPHONE 2

Hello, this is…	**Алло, это…** a-**lo** e-ta…
Can I speak to…?	**Позовите…** paza-**vi**-ti…
I've been cut off	**Меня прервали** mi-**nya** pri-**rva**-li
It's a bad line	**Плохо слышно** **plo**-kha **slisch**-na

YOU MAY HEAR:

Я пытаюсь вас соединить
ya pi-**ta**-yus' **vas** saidi-**nit'**

I'm trying to connect you

Соединяю
saidi-**nya**-yu

I'm putting you through

Подождите минутку
padazh-**di**-ti mi-**nut**-ku

Wait a minute

Занято
za-nita

It's engaged

Попытайтесь еще раз попозже
papi-**tai**-tis' i-**schcho** ras pa-**po**-zhi

Please try again later

Кто говорит?
kto gava-**rit**

Who's calling?

Извините, не тот номер
izvi-**ni**-ti ni **tot no**-mir

Sorry, wrong number

What time is it?	**Который час?** *ka-to-rii chas*
It's one o'clock (am/pm)	**Час (ночи/дня)** *chas (no-chi/dnya)*
It's two/three/four o'clock	**Два/три/четыре часа** *dva/tri/chi-ti-ri chi-sa*
It is five/six/etc o'clock	**Пять/шесть часов** *pyat'/schest' chi-sof*

8.00	**восемь часов** *vo-sim' chi-sof*	
8.05	**пять минут девятого** *pyat' mi-nut di-vya-tava*	
8.10	**десять минут девятого** *dye-sit' mi-nut di-vya-tava*	
8.15	**четверть девятого** *chye-tvirt' di-vya-tava*	
8.20	**двадцать минут девятого** *dva-tsat' mi-nut di-vya-tava*	
8.30	**половина девятого** *pala-vi-na di-vya-tava*	
8.40	**без двадцати девять** *biz dvatsa-ti dye-vit'*	
8.45	**без четверти девять** *bis chyet-virti dye-vit'*	
8.55	**без пяти девять** *bis pi-ti dye-vit'*	
12.00	**двенадцать часов** *dvi-na-tsat chi-sof*	

See also **NUMBERS**

TIME PHRASES

What time do you open/close?	**Во сколько вы открываетесь/ закрываетесь?** *va skol'-ka vi atkri-va-itis'/zakri-va-itis'*
Do we have time to visit the town?	**У нас есть время посмотреть город?** *unas yest' vrye-mya pasma-tryet' go-rat*
How long will it take to get there?	**Сколько туда добираться?** *skol'-ka tu-da dabi-rat-sa*
We arrived early/late	**Мы приехали рано/поздно** *mi pri-ye-khali ra-na/poz-na*
We must be back at the hotel before 11 o'clock	**Мы должны быть в гостинице до одиннадцати** *mi dal-zhni bit' vgas-ti-nitsi da a-di-natsati*
When does the coach leave in the morning?	**Во сколько отправляется автобус утром?** *va skol'-ka atprav-lya-itsa af-to-bus u-tram*

YOU MAY HEAR:

Экскурсия начинается в половине четвертого
iks-kur-siya nachi-na-itsa fpala-vi-ni chit-vyor-tava

The tour starts at about half past three

Музей открыт утром/после обеда
mu-zyei at-krit u-tram/pos-li a-bye-da

The museum is open in the morning/afternoon

Столик заказан на восемь тридцать вечера
sto-lik za-ka-zan na vo-sim' tri-tsat' vye-chira

The table is booked for 8.30 this evening

Streetwise

Restaurant service can be considerably improved with a gift of cigarettes or toiletries. When travelling in a group you may wish to pool resources to show thanks to the Intourist representative.

Sorry, I don't have any change

Извините, у меня нет сдачи
izvi-**nit**-ti umi-**nya** nyet zda-chi

Could you give me change of...?

Дайте мне сдачу...
dai-ti mnye **zda**-chu...

Is it usual to tip...?

Принято ли давать на чай...?
pri-nita li da-**vat'** na **chai**...

How much should I tip?

Сколько мне нужно дать на чай?
skol-ka mnye **nuzh**-na **dat'** na **chai**

Is the tip included?

Включено ли обслуживание?
vklyuchi-**no** li ap-**slu**-zhivaniye

Keep the change

Возьмите сдачу себе
vaz'-**mi**-ti **zda**-chu si-**bye**

Thank you very much

Спасибо вам большое
spa-**si**-ba vam bal'-**scho**-ye

See also **EATING OUT, HOTELS, TAXIS**

Streetwise

Public toilets which make a small charge are making a welcome recent appearance in city centres. There are few highway facilities for those travelling by road, so it is wise to carry toilet paper with you.

Where is the Gents'/
the Ladies'?

Где мужской/женский туалет?
*gdye muschs-**koi**/**zhens**-kii tua-**lyet***

Do you have to pay?

Здесь нужно платить?
*zdyes' **nuzh**-na pla-**tit'***

This toilet does not
flush

Этот унитаз не смывает
*e-tat uni-**tas** ni smi-**va**-it*

There is no toilet
paper/soap

Здесь нет туалетной бумаги/мыла
*zdyes' **nyet** tua-**lyet**-nai bu-**ma**-gi/**mi**-la*

Is there a toilet for
the disabled?

Здесь есть туалет для инвалидов?
*zdyes' **yest'** tua-**lyet** dlya inva-**li**-daf*

Are there facilities for
mothers with babies?

Здесь есть комната матери и ребенка?
*zdyes' **yest'** **kom**-nata **ma**-tiri i ri-**byon**-ka*

The door will not
close

Дверь не закрывается
*dvyer' ni zakri-**va**-itsa*

Is there a public
toilet nearby?

Есть ли поблизости туалет?
*yest' li pa-**bli**-zasti tua-**lyet***

Streetwise

Speed limits are 90 kph on the open road and 60 kph in urban areas. Most routes have signs in Cyrillic and Latin script. If you run into trouble, inform the Traffic Police ГАИ (ga-i). Inter-city night driving is forbidden to foreigners and there are few parking restrictions. Be sure to check with the AA or RAC if you take your own car.

What is the speed limit on this road?	**Какой лимит скорости на этой дороге?** *ka-koi li-mit sko-rasti na e-tai da-ro-gi*
Where can I park?	**Где можно запарковаться?** *gdye mozh-na zaparka-vat-sa*
Can I park overnight?	**Можно оставить здесь машину на ночь?** *mozh-na as-ta-vit' zdyes' ma-schi-nu na nach*

YOU MAY HEAR:

Вы превысили скорость
vi pri-vi-sili sko-rast'

You are driving too fast

Здесь парковка запрещена
zdyes' par-kof-ka zaprishchi-na

Parking is forbidden here

Вы развернулись в неположенном месте
vi razvir-nu-lis' vnipa-lo-zhinam myes-tye

You made an illegal U-turn

See also CAR HIRE, DRVING, EMERGENCIES, PETROL STATION

TRAIN TRAVEL

Streetwise

On long-distance trains first class consists of two adjacent beds to a compartment. Standard class contains two bunk beds. Men and women share the same compartment. Every carriage has a steward responsible for providing bedding and tea. There is a restaurant car.

Is this the train for…?	**Это поезд на…?** *e-ta **po**-ist na…*
Is this seat free?	**Это место свободно?** *e-ta **myes**-ta sva-**bod**-na*
I have a seat reservation	**Я забронировал(а) место** *ya zabra-**ni**-raval(a) **myes**-ta*
Can you help me put my suitcase on the luggage rack?	**Помогите мне положить чемодан на полку** *pama-**gi**-ti mnye pala-**zhit'** chima-**dan** na **pol**-ku*
May I open the window?	**Можно открыть окно?** *mozh-na at-**krit'** a-**kno***
What time do we get to…?	**Во сколько мы прибываем в…?** *va **skol'**-ka mi pribi-**va**-im v…*
Do we stop at…?	**Мы останавливаемся в…?** *mi asta-**nav**-livaimsya v…*
Where do I change for…?	**Где мне делать пересадку на…?** *gdye mnye **dye**-lat' piri-**sat**-ku na…*
Is there a buffet car/ restaurant car?	**Здесь есть вагон-ресторан?** *zdyes' **yest'** va-**gon**-rista-**ran***
Please tell me when to get off	**Скажите, когда мне выходить** *ska-**zhi**-ti kag-**da** mnye vikha-**dit'***

See also **LUGGAGE, RAILWAY STATION**

TRIPS AND EXCURSIONS

Streetwise

Intourist offers a wide selection of excellent tours at very reasonable prices, catering for all tastes, from general sightseeing tours of the cities to guided walks, architectural tours and sport, theatre, ballet and opera. See your Intourist representative or ask at the hotel Service Bureau.

Are there any sightseeing tours?	**У вас есть обзорные экскурсии?** uvas **yest'** ab-**zor**-nii iks-**kur**-sii
When is the bus tour of the town?	**Когда начинается автобусная экскурсия по городу?** kag-**da** nachi-**na**-itsa af-**to**-busnaya iks-**kur**-siya pa **go**-radu
How long does the tour take?	**Какая продолжительность экскурсии?** ka-**ka**-ya pradal-**zhi**-til'nast' iks-**kur**-sii
Are there any boat trips on the river/lake?	**Есть ли водные экскурсии по реке/озеру?** **yest'** li **vod**-nii iks-**kur**-sii pa ri-**kye**/**o**-ziru
Are there any guided tours of the cathedral?	**Есть ли в соборе экскурсии с гидом?** **yest'** li fsa-**bo**-ri iks-**kur**-sii zgi-**dam**
What is that building/ church?	**Что это за здание/церковь?** **schto** e-ta za **zda**-niye/**tsyer**-kaf'
Where can we eat?	**Где мы можем поесть?** **gdye** mi **mo**-zhim pa-**yest'**
Where do we stop for lunch?	**Где мы останавливаемся на обед?** **gdye** mi asta-**nav**-livaimsya naa-**byet**
Please stop the bus, my child is feeling sick!	**Остановите автобус, пожалуйста, моему ребенку плохо!** astana-**vi**-ti af-**to**-bus pa-**zha**-lusta mai-**mu** ri-**byon**-ku **plo**-kha

See also **FERRIES, SIGHTSEEING**

WEATHER

Be prepared for very cold weather in winter, from minus 12°C to minus 20°C. Fur hats with ear flaps can be bought from foreign currency shops. Summers tend to be short but hot.

It's a lovely day

Сегодня прекрасный день!
si-vod-nya pri-kras-nii dyen'

What dreadful weather!

Какая ужасная погода!
ka-ka-ya u-zhas-naya pa-go-da

It is raining/snowing

Идет дождь/снег
i-dyot doscht'/snyek

It's windy/foggy

На улице ветрено/туман
na u-litsi vye-trina/tu-man

Will it be cold tonight?

Сегодня ночью будет холодно?
si-vod-nya no-chyu bu-dit kho-ladna

Is it going to rain/ to snow?

Пойдет ли снег/дождь?
pai-dyot li snyek/doscht'

Will there be a frost?

Будет ли мороз?
bu-dit li ma-ros

Will there be a thunderstorm?

Будет ли гроза?
bu-dit li gra-za

Do you think it's going to be fine?

Вы думаете, будет отличная погода?
vi du-maiti bu-dit at-lich-naya pa-go-da

Is the weather going to change?

Будет ли меняться погода?
bu-dit li mi-nyat-sa pa-go-da

What is the temperature?

Какая температура?
ka-ka-ya timpira-tu-ra

WINES AND SPIRITS 1

Alcoholic beverages are popular in most parts of the former Soviet Union and are sold by the bottle or weight. A bottle of wine is about three-quarters of a litre, and a half bottle 350 grams. For a generous glass of wine, order 150 grams.

The best quality red and white wines come from the southern Republics of Georgia and Moldavia.

The most popular drink in restaurants and licensed snack bars is the local champagne **шампанское** (*scham-pans-kaye*), a pleasant sparkling white wine that comes in various grades of sweetness.

You may find the following terms useful:

wine	**вино**	*vi-**no***
white	**белое**	***bye**-laye*
red	**красное**	***kras**-naye*
dry	**сухое**	*su-**kho**-ye*
semi-dry	**полусухое**	*polusu-**kho**-ye*
sweet	**десертное**	*di-**sert**-naye*
beer	**пиво**	***pi**-va*
cognac	**коньяк**	*kan-**yak'***

Vodka **водка** (***vot**-ka*) is the undisputed national drink amongst Russians. It is invariably drunk neat, in one, as an accompaniment to a toast. There are many varieties including lemon and pepper. A standard 50-gram serving is the equivalent of a generous pub double! Be sure to follow it with a soft drink or some bread.

Russian beer can also be good. It is best when fresh. Armenian cognac is also well worth trying.

National and International brands of wines and spirits are available from the shops and bars of Intourist hotels for foreign currency.

до дна!
*da **dna***
cheers!

WINES AND SPIRITS 2

May I have the wine list, please?

Дайте, пожалуйста, список вин
dai-ti pa-*zha*-lusta *spi*-sak *vin*

Can you recommend a good red/white wine?

Какое хорошее красное/белое вино вы рекомендуете?
ka-*ko*-ye kha-*ro*-schiye **kras**-naye/**be**-laye vi-**no** vi rikamin-**du**-iti

Could I have a bottle/300g/50g?

Дайте мне бутылку/триста грамм/пятьдесят грамм
dai-ti mnye bu-*til*-ku/*tris*-ta gram/pit'di-*syat* gram

Please bring another glass

Принесите еще стакан, пожалуйста
prini-*si*-ti i-shcho sta-*kan* pa-*zha*-lusta

This wine is not chilled

Это вино не охлаждено
e-ta vi-**no** ni akhlazhdi-**no**

A lemon vodka, please

Лимонной водки, пожалуйста
li-**mon**-nai **vot**-ki pa-**zha**-lusta

A bottle of beer/champagne, please

Бутылку пива/шампанского, пожалуйста
bu-*til*-ku *pi*-va/scham-**pans**-kava pa-**zha**-lusta

A gin and tonic

Один джин с тоником
a-**din** dzhin *sto*-nikam

Your health!

Ваше здоровье!
va-schye sda-**rov**-ye

See also drinks **DRINKS, EATING OUT, MENU**

Streetwise

The Caucasus Mountains provide wonderful skiing opportunities. If you are staying in Moscow, why not visit the countryside for cross-country skiing or sledging?

Can we hire skis here?	**Можно здесь взять напрокат лыжи?** *mozh-na zdyes' vzyat' napra-kat li-zhi*
Could you adjust my bindings?	**Вы можете подогнать крепления?** *vi mo-zhiti pada-gnat' kri-plye-niya*
What are the snow conditions?	**В каком состоянии снег?** *fka-kom sasta-ya-nii snyek*
Which are the easiest runs?	**Какие трассы самые легкие?** *ka-ki-ye tra-si sa-mii lyokh-kii*
How do you get to the top?	**Как нам добраться до верха?** *kak nam da-brat-sa da vyer-kha*
Is there danger of avalanches?	**Есть ли опасность лавин?** *yest' li a-pas-nast' la-vin*
Where can we go skating?	**Где можно покататься на коньках?** *gdye mozh-na paka-tat-sa na kan'-kakh*
Is there a toboggan run?	**Здесь есть саночная трасса?** *zdyes' yest' sa-nachnaya tra-sa*
Can we book lessons here?	**Здесь можно записаться на уроки?** *zdyes' mozh-na zapi-sat-sa nau-ro-ki*
What is there to do at night?	**Куда здесь можно пойти вечером?** *ku-da zdyes' mozh-na pai-ti vye-chiram*

abbey монастырь *manas-tir'*

about о; около *o; o-kala;* **a book about Moscow** книга о Москве *kni-ga a Mas-kyve;* **about ten o'clock** около десяти часов *o-kala disi-ti chi-sof*

above над *nat;* **above me** надо мной *nada mnoi*

accident (catastrophe) несчастный случай *ni-shchas-nii slu-chii*

accommodation жилье *zhil-yo*

ache vb болеть *bal-yet';* **my head aches** у меня болит голова *umi-nya ba-lit gala-va*

actor артист *ar-tist*

adaptor (electrical) адаптор *a-dap-tar*

address адрес *a-dris*

adhesive tape клейкая лента *klei-kaya lyen-ta*

admission charge входная плата *fkhad-na-ya pla-ta*

adult взрослый *vzros-lii*

advance: in advance авансом *a-van-sam*

after после *po-sli*

afternoon после обеда *po-sli a-bye-da*

again опять *a-pyat'*

ago: a week ago неделю назад *ni-dye-lyu na-zat*

air-conditioning кондиционер *kanditsia-nyer*

airline авиалиния *avia-li-niya*

air mail авиапочта *avia-poch-ta*

airport аэропорт *aero-port*

aisle проход *pra-hot*

alarm (emergency) тревога *tri-vo-ga*

alarm clock будильник *bu-dil'-nik*

alcohol алкоголь *alka-gol'*

all (everything) всё *fsyo;* (everyone) все *fsye*

allergic to аллергия на *alir-gi-ya na*

allowance (customs) норма беспошлинного груза *nor-ma bis-posch-linava gru-za*

all right (agreed) все хорошо *fsyo hara-scho;* **are you all right?** у вас все в порядке? *uvas fsyo fpa-ryat-ki*

almost почти *pach-ti*

also тоже *to-zhe*

always всегда *fsig-da*

am (to be) see **GRAMMAR**

ambulance скорая помощь *sko-raya po-mashch*

America Америка *a-mye-rika*

American m/f/adj американец/ американка/американский *amiri-ka-nits/amiri-kan-ka/amiri-kan-skii*

anaesthetic анестетик *anis-te-tik*

anchor якорь *ya-kar'*

and и *i*

anorak куртка *kurt-ka*

another другой *dru-goi;* **another beer?** еще пива? *i-shcho pi-va*

antibiotics антибиотики *antibi-o-tiki*

antifreeze антифриз *anti-fris*

antiseptic антисептик *anti-sep-tik*

any любой *lyu-boi*

anyway все равно *fsyo rav-no*

anywhere где-нибудь *gdye-nibut'*

apartment квартира *kvar-ti-ra*

apple яблоко *yab-laka*

appointment встреча *fstrye-cha*

WORDS

apricot абрикос *abri-kos*

are (to be) see **GRAMMAR**

arm рука *ru-ka*

army армия *ar-miya*

arrivals (by air) прилет *pri-lyot*

arrive приезжать *priye-zhat'*

art искусство *is-kust-va*; **art gallery** картинная галерея *kar-tin-aya gali-rye-ya*

ashtray пепельница *pye-pil'nitsa*

aspirin аспирин *aspi-rin*

asthma астма *ast-ma*

at: at home дома *do-ma*

aubergine баклажан *bakla-zhan*

Australia Австралия *afs-tra-liya*

Australian m/f/adj австралиец/ австралийка/австралийский *afstra-li-its/afstra-lii-ka/afstra-lii-skii*

automatic автоматический *aftama-ti-chiskii*

autumn осень *o-sin'*

avalanche лавина *la-vi-na*

awful ужасный *u-zhas-nii*

baby ребенок *ri-byo-nak*

baby food детское питание *dyet-skaye pi-ta-niye*

baby-sitter няня *nya-nya*

back (of body) спина *spi-na*

backpack рюкзак *ryuk-zak*

bacon бекон *bi-kon*

bad плохой *pla-hoi*

bag (small) сумка *sum-ka*

baggage багаж *ba-gasch*

baggage reclaim выдача багажа *vi-dacha baga-zha*

baker's булочная *bu-lachnaya*

balcony балкон *bal-kon*

ball мяч *myach*

banana банан *ba-nan*

band (musical) оркестр *ar-kyestr*

bandage бинт *bint*

bank банк *bank*

bar бар *bar*

barbecue шашлык *schasch-lik*

barber парикмахер *parik-ma-khir*

basket корзина *kar-zi-na*

bath ванна *van-na*; **to take a bath** принимать ванну *prini-mat' van-nu*

bathing cap купальная шапочка *ku-pal'-naya scha-pachka*

bathroom ванная *van-naya*

battery (car) батарея *bata-rye-ya*; (radio, etc) батарейка *bata-ryei-ka*

be (to be) see **GRAMMAR**

beach пляж *plyasch*

bean (haricot) фасоль *fa-sol'*; (coffee) бобы *ba-bi*; (green) горох *ga-rokh*

beautiful красивый *kra-si-vii*

bed кровать *kra-vat'*

bedding постельное белье *pa-styel'-naye bil-yo*

bedroom спальня *spal'-nya*

beef говядина *ga-vya-dina*

beer пиво *pi-va*

beetroot свекла *svyok-la*

before (time) до *do*; (place) перед *pye-rit*

begin начинать *nachi-nat'*

behind сзади *zzadi*

below ниже *ni-zhi*

belt пояс *po-is*

beside рядом *rya*-dam

best лучший *lut*-schii

better (than) лучше чем *lut*-schi chyem

between между *myezh*-du

bicycle велосипед vilasi-*pyet*

big большой bal'-*schoi*

bigger больше *bol'*-schi

bill счет *shchot*

bin мусорное ведро *mu*-sarnaye vid-ro

binoculars бинокль bi-*nokl'*

bird птица *pti*-tsa

birthday день рождения *dyen'* razh-*dye*-nya; **happy birthday!** с днем рождения! *zdnyom* razh-*dye*-nya

bit кусочек ku-*so*-chik; **a bit of** чуть-чуть chut'-*chut'*

bitten: I have been bitten я покусан(а) ya pa-*ku*-san(a)

bitter горький *gor'*-kii

black черный *chyor*-nii

blackcurrant черная смородина *chyor*-naya sma-*ro*-dina

blanket одеяло adi-*ya*-la

blocked засорена za-*so*-rina

blood group группа крови *gru*-pa *kro*-vi

blouse блуза *blu*-za

blow-dry уложить ula-*zhit'*

blue голубой galu-*boi*

boarding card посадочный талон pa-*sa*-dachnii ta-*lon*

boarding house пансион pansi-*on*

boat лодка *lot*-ka

boat trip морская прогулка *mars*-ka-ya pra-*gul*-ka

boiled вареный va-*ryo*-nii

book¹ *n* книга *kni*-ga

book² *vb* заказывать za-*ka*-zivat'

booking делать заказ *dye*-lat' za-*kas*

booking office (railway, airlines) заказ билетов za-*kas* bi-*lye*-taf

bookshop книжный магазин *knizh*-nii maga-*zin*

boots сапоги sapa-*gi*

border граница gra-*ni*-tsa

both *m/f* оба/обе *o*-ba/o-*bi*

bottle бутылка bu-*til*-ka

bottle opener штопор *schto*-par

box коробка ka-*rop*-ka

box office (театральная) касса (tiat-*ral'*-naya) *ka*-sa

boy мальчик *mal'*-chik

boyfriend друг *druk*

bra лифчик *lif*-chik

brake fluid тормозная жидкость tarmaz-*na*-ya *zhit*-kast'

brakes тормоза tarma-*za*

brandy брэнди; коньяк *bren*-di; kan'-*yak*

bread хлеб *khlyep*

breakable хрупкий *khrup*-kii

breakdown авария a-*va*-riya

breakdown van техническая помощь tikh-*ni*-chiskaya *po*-mashch

breakfast завтрак *zaf*-trak

briefcase портфель part-*fyel'*

bring приносить prina-*sit'*

Britain Британия bri-*ta*-niya

British *m/f/adj* британец/британка/ британский bri-*ta*-nits/bri-*tan*-ka/bri-*tans*-kii

broken сломанный *slo-manii*

broken down (machine, car) сломалась *sla-ma-las'*

brooch брошь *brosch*

brother брат *brat*

brown коричневый *ka-rich-nivii*

brush щетка *shchot-ka*

Brussels sprouts брюссельская капуста *bryu-sel's-kaya ka-pus-ta*

bucket ведро *vi-dro*

buffet буфет *bu-fyet*

buffet car вагон-ресторан *va-gon-rista-ran*

bulb лампочка *lam-pachka*

bun булочка *bu-lachka*

bureau de change обменный пункт *ab-myen-nii punkt*

burst лопнуть *lop-nut'*

bus автобус *af-to-bus*

bus station автовокзал *aftavag-zal*

bus stop автобусная остановка *af-to-busnaya asta-nof-ka*

bus tour автобусная экскурсия *af-to-busnaya iks-kur-siya*

business бизнес *biz-nes*

busy занят *za-nyat*

but но *no*

butcher's мясной магазин *mis-noi maga-zin*

butter масло *ma-sla*

button пуговица *pu-gavitsa*

buy покупать *paku-pat'*

by (near) около *o-kala*

bypass (by car) объезд *ab-yest*

cabaret кабаре *kaba-re*

cabbage капуста *ka-pus-ta*

cablecar фуникулер *funiku-lyor*

café кафе *ka-fe*

cagoule ветровка *vi-trof-ka*

cake торт *tort*

call[1] *vb* (shout) звать *zvat'*; (on telephone) звонить *zva-nit'*

call[2] *n* (on telephone) звонок *zva-nok*; **a long-distance call** междугородный разговор *myezhduga-rod-nii razga-vor*

calm спокойный *spa-koi-nii*

camera (photo) фотоаппарат *fotaapa-rat*; (video) видеокамера *vidio-ka-mira*

camp лагерь *la-gir'*

camp site кемпинг *kyem-pink*

can[1] *n* (food) банка *ban-ka*; (oil) канистра *ka-nist-ra*

can[2] *vb* (to be able) мочь *moch*

Canada Канада *ka-na-da*

Canadian *m/f/adj* канадец/канадка/канадский *ka-na-dits/ka-nat-ka/ka-nats-kii*

cancel отменять *atmi-nyat'*

canoe байдарка *bai-dar-ka*

canoeing ходить на байдарке *kha-dit'na bai-dar-kye*

can opener консервный нож *kan-syerv-nii nosch*

car машина *ma-schi-na*

carafe графин *gra-fin*

caravan караван *kara-van*

carburettor карбюратор *karbyu-ra-tar*

card (greetings) открытка *at-krit-ka*; (playing) карта *kar-ta*; **to play cards** играть в карты *i-grat' fkhar-ti*

cardigan кофта *kof-ta*

WORDS

careful осторожный *asta-rozh-nii*

car park стоянка машин *sta-yan-ka ma-schin*

carpet ковер *ka-vyor*

carriage *(railway)* вагон *va-gon*

carrot морковь *mar-kof'*

carry нести *nis'-ti*

car wash мойка машин *moi-ka ma-schin*

case *(suitcase)* чемодан *chima-dan*

cash[1] *vb (cheque)* получить деньги по чеку *palu-chit' dyen'-gi pa chye-ky*

cash[2] *n* наличные деньги *na-lich-nii dyen'-gi*

cash desk касса *ka-sa*

cashier кассир *ka-sir*

casino казино *kazi-no*

cassette кассета *ka-sye-ta*

castle замок *za-mak*

catch ловить *la-vit'*

cathedral собор *sa-bor*

Catholic *adj* католический *kata-li-chiskii*

cauliflower цветная капуста *tsvit-na-ya ka-pus-ta*

cave пещера *pi-shche-ra*

celery сельдерей *sil'di-ryei*

cemetery кладбище *klad-bishche*

centimetre сантиметр *santi-myetr*

central центральный *tsint-ral'-nii*

centre центр *tsentr*

certain *(sure)* уверен *u-vye-rin*

certificate удостоверение *udastavi-rye-niye*

chain цепь *tsep'*

chair стул *stul*

chairlift подъемник *pad-yom-nik*

chalet дача *da-cha*

champagne шампанское *scham-pans-kaye*

change[1] *n (money)* сдача *zda-cha*

change[2] *vb (money)* менять *mi-nyat'* ; *(clothes)* переодеваться *piriadi-vat-sa*

changing room раздевалка *razdi-val-ka*

chapel часовня *chi-sov-nya*

charge плата *pla-ta*

cheap дешево *dyo-schiva*

cheaper дешевле *di-schev-li*

check проверять *pravi-ryat'*

check in *vb (at hotel, airport)* регистрироваться *rigist-ri-ravatsa*

check-in desk служба приема *sluzh-ba pri-yo-ma*

cheer up! Не грусти! *ni grus-ti*

cheerio Пока! *pa-ka*

cheers На здоровье! *na zda-rov-ye*

cheese сыр *sir*

chemist's аптека *ap-tye-ka*

cheque чек *chek*

cheque book чековая книжка *chye-kavaya knisch-ka*

cheque card чековая карточка *chye-kavaya kar-tachka*

cherry вишня *visch-nya*

chess шахматы *schakh-mati*

chestnut каштан *kasch-tan*

chewing gum жвачка *zhvach-ka*

chicken курица *ku-ritsa*

child ребенок *ri-byo-nak*

children дети *dye-ti*

chilled: is the wine chilled? вино холодное? *vi-***no** *kha-***lod**-*naye*

chilli жгучий перец *zhgu-chii* **pye**-*rits*

chips чипсы **chip**-*si*

chocolate шоколад *shaka-***lat**

chocolates шоколадные конфеты *shaka-***lad**-*nii kan-***fye**-*ti*

Christmas Рождество *razhdist-***vo**

church церковь *tser-kaf'*

cider сидр *sidr*

cigar сигара *si-***ga**-*ra*

cigarette сигарета *siga-***rye**-*ta*

cigarette papers бумага для папирос *bu-***ma**-*ga dlya papi-***ros**

cinema кино *ki-***no**

circus цирк *tsirk*

city город **go**-*rat*

clean¹ adj чистый **chis**-*tii*

clean² vb убирать *ubi-***rat'**

cleansing cream очищающий крем *achi-***shcha**-*yushchii* **kryem**

client клиент *kli-yent*

climbing альпинизм *al'pi-***nizm**

climbing boots альпинистские ботинки *alpi-***nis**-*kii ba-***tin**-*ki*

cloakroom гардероб *gardi-***rop**

clock часы *chi-si*

close¹ adj (near) близкий **blis**-*kii*

close² vb закрывать *zakri-***vat'**

closed закрыто *za-***kri**-*ta*

cloth (material) материя *ma-***tye**-*riya*

clothes одежда *a-***dyezh**-*da*

clothespeg прищепка *pri-***shchep**-*ka*

cloudy облачно **o**-*blachna*

cloves гвоздика *gvaz-***di**-*ka*

club клуб *klup*

coach (bus) междугородный автобус *myezhduga-***rod**-*nii af-to-bus*

coach trip автобусная поездка *af-to-busnaya pa-***yest**-*ka*

coast побережье *pabi-***rye**-*zhye*

coastguard спасатель *spa-***sa**-*til'*

coat пальто *pal'-***to**

coat hanger вешалка *vye-***schalka**

cocktail коктейль *kak-***tel'**

cocoa какао *ka-***kao**

coconut кокос *ka-***kos**

coffee кофе *ko-fye*; **white coffee** кофе с молоком *ko-fye smala-***kom**; **black coffee** черный кофе *chyor-nii ko-fye*

coin монета *ma-***nye**-*ta*

Coke ® кока-кола *ko-ka ko-la*

cold¹ n холод *kho-lat*; **I have a cold** я простужен(а) *ya pra-***stu**-*zhin(a)*

cold² adj холодный *kha-***lod**-*nii*; **I'm cold** мне холодно *mnye* **kho**-*ladna*

colour цвет *tsvyet*

comb расческа *ras-***chyos**-*ka*

come приходить *prikha-***dit'**; (by car) приезжать *priye-***zhat'**; **to come back** возвращаться *vazvra-***shchat**-*sa*; **to come in** входить *fkha-***dit'**; **come in!** войдите! *vai-***di**-*ti*

comfortable удобный *u-***dob**-*nii*

company кампания *kam-***pa**-*niya*

compartment купе *ku-***pe**

complain жаловаться *zha-lavatsa*

compulsory обязательный *abi-***za**-*til'nii*

computer компьютер *kam-***pyu**-*ter*

concert концерт *kan-***tsert**

condensed milk сгущеное

молоко zgu-**shcho**-naye mala-**ko**

conditioner бальзам для волос bal'-**zam** dlya va-**los**

conductor (on bus) кондуктор kan-**duk**-tar

conference конференция kanfi-**ryen**-tsiya

confirm подтвердить patvir-**dit'**

congratulations! поздравляю! pazdrav-**lya**-yu

connection связь svyas'

constipation запор za-**por**

consulate консульство **kon**-sul'stva

contact vb связаться с svi-**zat**-sa s

contact lens cleaner очиститель контактных линз achis-**ti**-til' kan-**takt**-nikh lins

contact lenses контактные линзы kan-**takt**-nii **lin**-zi

contraceptive контрацептив kantratsip-**tif**

cook готовить ga-**to**-vit'

cool прохладный pra-**khlad**-nii

copy[1] n копия **ko**-piya

copy[2] vb копировать ka-**pi**-ravat'

corkscrew штопор **schto**-par

corner угол **u**-gal

cosmetics косметика kas-**mye**-tika

cost стоить **sto**-it'; **how much does it/do they cost?** сколько это стоит? **skol**'-ka **e**-ta sto-it

cotton хлопок **khlo**-pak

cotton wool вата **va**-ta

couchette полка **pol**-ka

cough кашель **ka**-schil'

country страна stra-**na**

countryside сельская местность **syel's**-kaya **myes**-nast'

couple (2 people) пара **pa**-ra

courgette кабачки kabach-**ki**

courier курьер kur-**yer**

course (of meal) блюдо **blyu**-da

cover charge входная плата fkhad-**na**-ya **pla**-ta

cow корова ka-**ro**-va

crab краб **krap**

crash n катастрофа katast-**ro**-fa

cream (lotion) крем **kryem**; (on milk) сливки **slif**-ki

credit card кредитная карточка kri-**dit**-naya **kar**-tachka

crisps хрустящий картофель khrus-**tya**-schii kar-**to**-fil'

cross (road) переходить pirikha-**dit'**

crossroads перекресток piri-**kryos**-tak

crowded переполненный piri-**pol**-ninii

cruise круиз kru-**is**

cucumber огурец agu-**ryets**

cup чашка **chasch**-ka

cupboard шкаф **schkaf**

curlers бигуди bigu-**di**

currant смородина sma-**ro**-dina

current (sea) течение ti-**chye**-niye

cushion подушка pa-**dusch**-ka

customs таможня ta-**mozh**-nya

cut[1] n порез pa-**ryes**

cut[2] vb резать **rye**-zat'; **we've been cut off** нас разъединили **nas** razyedi-**ni**-li

cycling ездить на велосипеде **yez**-dit' na vilasi-**pye**-di

damage n ущерб u-**shcherp**

damp сырой si-**roi**

dance[1] n танец **ta**-nits

dance[2] vb танцевать tantsi-**vat'**

dangerous опасный a-**pas**-nii

dark темный **tyom**-nii

date число **chis**-lo

date of birth дата рождения **da**-ta razh-**dye**-niya

daughter дочь **doch**

day день **dyen'**

dear дорогой dara-**goi**

decaffeinated без кофеина bis kafi-**i**-na

deck chair шезлонг schiz-**lonk**

declare заявлять sayev-**lyat'**

deep глубокий glu-**bo**-kii

deep freeze морозилка mara-**zil**-ka

defrost разморозить razma-**ro**-zit'

delay n задержка za-**dyersch**-ka

delicious восхитительный vaskhi-**ti**-til'nii

dentist дантист dan-**tist**

dentures (зубные) протезы (zub-**nii**) pra-**te**-zi

deodorant деодорант deodo-**rant**

department store универмаг univir-**mak**

departure lounge зал отправления **zal** atprav-**lye**-niya

departures отправление atprav-**lye**-niye

deposit залог za-**lok**

dessert десерт di-**syert**

details детали di-**ta**-li

detergent моющее средство **mo**-yushcheye **sryets**-tva

detour (by car) объезд ab-**yest**

develop развивать razvi-**vat'**

diabetic диабетический diabi-**ti**-chiskii

dialling code телефонный код tili-**fon**-nii kot

diamond бриллиант brili-**ant**

diarrhoea понос pa-**nos**

diary дневник dniv-**nik**

dictionary словарь sla-**var'**

diesel дизель di-**zil'**

diet диета di-**ye**-ta

different другой dru-**goi**

difficult трудный **trud**-nii

dining room столовая sta-**lo**-vaya

dinner ужин **u**-zhin

direct (train, etc) прямой pri-**moi**

directory справочник **spra**-vachnik

dirty грязный **gryaz**-nii

disabled нетрудоспособный nitrudaspa-**sob**-nii

disco дискотека diska-**tye**-ka

discount скидка **skit**-ka

dish блюдо **blyu**-da

dishwasher посудомоечная машина pasuda-**mo**-ichnaya ma-**schi**-na

disinfectant дезинфицирующее средство dizinfi-**tsi**-ruyushchiye **sryet**-stva

distilled water дистиллированная вода distili-**ro**-vanaya va-**da**

divorced в разводе v raz-**vo**-di

dizzy: I feel dizzy у меня кружится голова umi-**nya** kru-**zhitsa** gala-**va**

do делать **dye**-lat'

doctor доктор; врач **dok**-tar; **vrach**

documents документы *daku-myen-ti*

doll кукла *kuk-la*

dollar доллар *do-lar*

door дверь *dvyer'*

double двойной *dvai-noi*

double bed двухспальная кровать *dvukh-spal'-naya kra-vat'*

double room комната на двоих *kom-nata na dva-ikh*

doughnut пончик *pon-chik*

down вниз *vnis*; **to go down** (downstairs) спускаться *spus-kat-sa*

downstairs внизу *vni-zu*

draught (of air) сквозняк *skvaz'-nyak*

dress[1] n платье *pla-tye*

dress[2] vb (to get dressed) одеться *a-dyet-sa*

dressing (for food) приправа *pri-pra-va*

drink[1] n напиток *na-pi-tak*

drink[2] vb пить *pit'*

drinking chocolate жидкий шоколад *zhit-kii schaka-lat*

drinking water питьевая вода *pitye-va-ya va-da*

drive водить машину *va-dit' ma-schi-nu*

driver (of car) водитель *va-di-til'*

driving licence (водительские) права *(va-di-til'skii) pra-va*

drunk пьяный *pya-nii*

dry[1] adj сухой *su-khoi*

dry[2] vb сушить *su-schit'*

dry cleaner's химчистка *khim-chist-ka*

duck утка *ut-ka*

due: when is the train due? Когда прибывает поезд? *kag-da pribi-va-it po-ist*

dummy пустышка *pus-tisch-ka*

during во время *va vrye-mya*

duty-free безпошлинный *bis-posch-linii*

duty-free shop беспошлинный магазин *bis-posch-linii maga-zin*

duvet перина *pi-ri-na*

dynamo динамо; генератор *di-na-ma; gini-ra-tor*

each каждый *kazh-dii*

ear ухо *u-kha*

earache боль в ухе *bol' vu-khi*

earlier раньше *ran'-schi*

early рано *ra-na*

earrings серьги *syer'-gi*

east восток *vas-tok*

Easter Пасха *pas-kha*

easy легкий *lyokh-kii*

eat есть *yest'*

eel угорь *u-gar'*

egg яйцо *yai-tso*; **boiled eggs** яйца всмятку *yai-tsa fsmyat-ku*; **fried egg** яичница *ya-ich-nitsa*; **hard-boiled egg** яйцо вкрутую *yai-tso fkru-tu-yu*

either любой *lyu-boi*; **either... or...** или... или... *i-li... i-li*

elastic резинка *ri-zin-ka*

elastic band резинка *ri-zin-ka*

electric электрический *ilik-tri-chiskii*

electrician электрик *i-lyek-trik*

electricity электричество *ilik-tri-chistva*

electric razor электробритва
ilyektra-brit-va

embassy посольство *pa-sol'-stva*

emergency тревога *tri-vo-ga*

empty пустой *pus-toi*

end конец *ka-nyets*

engaged¹ *(to be married)* обручен
abru-chyon

engaged² *(phone, toilet)* занят *za-
nyat*

engine мотор *ma-tor*

England Англия *an-gliya*

English *m/f/adj* англичанин/
англичанка/английский *angli-
cha-nin/angli-chan-ka/an-gli-skii*

enjoy: I enjoyed the tour мне
понравилась поездка *mnye pa-
nra-vilas' pa-yest-ka;* **I enjoy
swimming** я люблю плавать *ya
lyu-blyu pla-vat'*

enough достаточно *das-ta-tachna*

enquiry desk справочное *spra-
vachnaye*

entertainment развлечение *razvli-
chye-niye*

entrance вход *fkhot*

entrance fee входная плата *fhad-
na-ya pla-ta*

envelope конверт *kan-vyert*

equipment оборудование *aba-ru-
davaniye*

escalator эскалатор *iska-la-tor*

especially специально *spitsi-al'-na*

essential важный *vazh-nii*

Europe Европа *yev-ro-pa*

evening вечер *vye-chir;* **in the
evening** вечером *vye-chiram*

evening meal ужин *u-zhin*

every каждый *kazh-dii*

everyone все *fsye*

everything всё *fsyo*

excellent отличный *at-lich-nii*

except кроме *kro-mi*

excess luggage перевес багажа
piri-vyes baga-zha

exchange¹ *n* обмен *ab-myen*

exchange² *vb* обменивать *ab-mye-
nivat'*

exchange rate курс *kurs*

excursion экскурсия *iks-kur-siya*

excuse: excuse me! *(sorry)*
извините! *izvi-ni-ti;* *(when passing)*
разрешите! *razri-schi-ti*

exhaust pipe выхлопная труба
vikhlap-na-ya tru-ba

exhibition выставка *vi-stafka*

exit выход *vi-khat*

expensive дорогой *dara-goi*

expert эксперт *iks-pyert*

expire *(ticket, passport)*
оканчиваться *a-kan-chivatsa*

express¹ *n* *(train)* скорый поезд;
экспресс *sko-rii po-ist; iks-pryes*

express² *adj* *(parcel, etc)* срочный
sroch-nii

extra *(spare)* запасной *zapas-noi;*
(more) экстра *eks-tra*

eye liner карандаш для глаз
karan-dasch dlya glas

eyes глаза *gla-za*

eye shadow тени для век *tye-ni
dlya vyek*

facilities удобства *y-dop-stva*

faint падать в обморок *pa-dat'
vob-marak*

fair *(fun fair)* ярмарка *yar-marka;* *(hair)* светлый *svyet-lii*

fall падать *pa-dat'*

family семья *si-mya*

famous известный *iz-vyes-nii*

fan *(electric)* вентилятор *vinti-lya-tar;* *(supporter)* болельщик *ba-lyel'-shchik*

fan belt ремень вентилятора *ri-myen' vinti-lya-tara*

far далеко *dali-ko*

fare плата *pla-ta*

farm ферма *fyer-ma*

farmhouse *(wooden)* изба *iz-ba*

fast быстрый *bis-trii*

fat *n* сало *sa-la*

father папа *pa-pa*

fault *(defect)* дефект *di-fyekt;* **it's not my fault** это не моя вина *e-ta ni ma-ya vi-na*

favourite любимый *lyu-bi-mii*

feed кормить *kar-mit'*

feel чувствовать *chust-vavat';* **I don't feel well** мне не хорошо *mnye ni hara-scho;* **I feel sick** меня тошнит *mi-nya tasch-nit*

ferry паром *pa-rom*

festival фестиваль *fisti-val'*

fetch *(bring)* приносить *prina-sit';* *(go and get)* принеси *prini-si*

fever жар *zhar*

few/a few несколько *nyes-kal'ka*

fiancé жених *zhi-nikh*

fiancée невеста *ni-vyes-ta*

field поле *po-lye*

fill заполнять *zapal-nyat';* **to fill up** *(container)* заполнять *zapal-nyat';* **fill it up!** залейте до верху! *za-lei-ti do vyer-khu*

fillet филе *fi-lye*

filling *(in tooth)* пломба *plom-ba*

film *(cinema)* фильм *fil'm;* *(for camera)* пленка *plyon-ka*

filter фильтр *fil'tr*

filter-tipped с фильтром *sfil't-ram*

finish кончать *kan-chat'*

fire огонь *a-gon';* **fire!** пожар! *pa-zhar*

fire brigade пожарная команда *pa-zhar-naya ka-man-da*

fire extinguisher огнетушитель *agnitu-schi-til'*

fireworks салют *sa-lyut*

first первый *pyer-vii*

first aid первая помощь *pyer-vaya po-mashch*

first class первый класс *pyer-vii klas*

first floor первый этаж *pyer-vii i-tasch*

first name имя *i-mya*

fish[1] *n* рыба *ri-ba*

fish[2] *vb* ловить рыбу *la-vit' ri-bu*

fit[1] *vb* подходить *patka-dit;* **it doesn't fit me** мне это не подходит *mnye e-ta ni pat-kho-dit*

fit[2] *adj (medical)* здоровый *zda-ro-vii*

fix назначать *nazna-chat'*

fizzy газированный *gazi-ro-vanii*

flash вспышка *fspisch-ka*

flask термос *ter-mas*

flat *(apartment)* квартира *kvar-ti-ra*

flat tyre спущенная шина *spu-shchinaya schi-na*

flight полет *pa-lyot*

floor (of building) этаж *i-tasch*; (of room) пол *pol*

flour мука *mu-ka*

flower цветок *tsvi-tok*

flu грипп *grip*

fly (insect) муха *mu-kha*

fog туман *tu-man*

follow следовать *slye-davat'*

food еда *ye-da*

food poisoning пищевое отравление *pishchi-vo-ye atrav-lye-niye*

foot ступня *stup-nya*; (measure) = **30.48 см**

football футбол *fut-bol*

for для *dlya*

foreign иностранный *ina-stra-nii*

forest лес *lyes*

forget забывать *zabi-vat'*

fork вилка *vil-ka*; (in road) развилка *ras-vil-ka*

fortnight две недели *dvye-ni-dye-li*

fountain фонтан *fan-tan*

France Франция *fran-tsiya*

free (not occupied) свободный *sva-bod-nii*; (costing nothing) бесплатный *bis-plat-nii*

freezer морозилка *mara-zil-ka*

French m/f/adj француз/француженка/французский *fran-tsus/fran-tsu-zhinka/fran-tsus-kii*

french beans фасоль *fa-sol'*

frequent частый *chas-tii*

fresh свежий *svye-zhii*

fridge холодильник *khala-dil'-nik*

fried жареный *zha-rinii*

friend (male) друг *druk*; (female)

подруга *pa-dru-ga*

from из *is*

front: in front перед *pye-rit*

frozen (food) замороженый *zama-ro-zhinii*

fruit фрукты *fruk-ti*

fruit juice (фруктовый) сок *(fruk-to-vii) sok*

fruit salad фруктовый салат *(fruk-to-vii) sa-lat*

frying pan сковорода *skavara-da*

fuel топливо *top-liva*

fuel pump бензоколонка *binzaka-lon-ka*

full полный *pol-nii*

full board полный пансион *pol-nii pansi-on*

funny (amusing) смешной *smisch-noi*; (strange) странный *stra-nii*

fur мех *myekh*

fuse предохранитель *pridakhra-ni-til'*

gallery галерея *gali-rye-ya*

gallon see **CONVERSION CHARTS**

gambling азартные игры *a-zart-nii i-gri*

game игра *i-gra*

garage гараж *ga-rasch*

garden сад *sat*

garlic чеснок *chis-nok*

gas газ *gas*

gas cylinder газовый баллон *ga-zavii ba-lon*

gate ворота *va-ro-ta*

gears скорости *sko-rasti*

gentleman господин *gaspa-din*

Gents' мужской туалет muschs-**koi** tua-**lyet**

genuine (leather, silver) настоящий nasta-**ya**-shchii

German m/f/adj немец/немка/ немецкий **nye**-mits/**nyem**-ka/ni-**myets**-kii

Germany Германия gir-**ma**-niya

get (obtain) доставать dasta-**vat'** ; (receive) получать palu-**chat'** ; (fetch) приносить prina-**sit'** ; **to get into** (house, clothes) залезть zali-**zat'** ; **to get into the bus** садиться в автобус sa-**dit**-sa vaf-to-bus; **to get off** (bus, etc) сходить skha-**dit'** ; **to get up** вставать fsta-**vat'**

gift подарок pa-**da**-rak

gift shop подарочный магазин pa-da-rachnii maga-**zin**

gin джин dzhin

ginger имбирь im-**bir'**

girl (little) девочка **dye**-vachka; (young) девушка **dye**-vushka

girlfriend подруга pa-**dru**-ga

give давать da-**vat'** ; **to give back** отдавать otda-**vat'**

glass (for drinking) стакан sta-**kan** ; (substance) стекло sti-**klo**

glasses очки ach-**ki**

gloves перчатки pir-**chat**-ki

glucose глюкоза glyu-**ko**-za

glue клей **klei**

go идти it-**ti** ; **to go back** возвращаться vazvra-**shchat**-sa; **to go down** (downstairs, etc) спускаться spus-**kat**-sa; **to go in** входить fkha-**dit'** ; **to go out** (leave) выходить vikha-**dit'** ; **to go up** подниматься padni-**mat**-sa

goat козел ka-**zyol**

goggles защитные очки za-**shchit**-nii ach-**ki**

gold золото **zo**-lata

golf гольф **gol'**f

golf course площадка для гольфа pla-**shchat**-ka dlya **gol'**-fa

good хороший kha-**ro**-shii

good afternoon добрый день **dob**-rii dyen'

goodbye до свидания dasvi-**da**-niya

good evening добрый вечер **dob**-rii **vye**-chir

good morning доброе утро **do**-braye **u**-tra

good night спокойной ночи spa-**koi**-nai **no**-chi

goods товары ta-va-ri

goose гусь **gus'**

gram грамм **gram**

grandfather дедушка **dye**-duschka

grandmother бабушка **ba**-buschka

grapefruit грейпфрут greip-**frut**

grapefruit juice грейпфрутовый сок greip-**fru**-tavii **sok**

grapes виноград vina-**grat**

grass трава tra-**va**

gravy подливка pad-**lif**-ka

greasy жирный zhir-nii

green зеленый zi-**lyo**-nii

grey серый **sye**-rii

grilled гриль **gril'**

grocer's бакалея baka-**lye**-ya

ground земля zyem-lya

ground floor первый этаж **pyer**-vii i-**tasch**

group группа **gru**-pa

group passport групповой паспорт *grupa-voi pas-part*

guarantee n гарантия *ga-ran-tiya*

guard (on train) кондуктор *kan-duk-tar*

guest гость *gost'*

guesthouse гостиница *gas-ti-nitsa*

guide[1] n гид *git*

guide[2] vb руководить *rukava-dit'*

guidebook путеводитель *putiva-di-til'*

guided tour экскурсия *iks-kur-siya*

gym shoes спортивные тапочки *spar-tiv-nii ta-pachki*

hair волосы *vo-lasi*

hairbrush щетка для волос *shot-ka dlya va-los*

haircut стрижка *strisch-ka*

hairdresser парикмахер *parik-ma-kher*

hairdryer фен *fyen*

hair spray лак для волос *lak dlya va-los*

half половина *pala-vi-na*

half board полупансион *polupansi-on*

half fare половинная стоимость *pala-vi-naya sto-imast'*

ham ветчина *vichi-na*

hand рука *ru-ka*

handbag (дамская) сумочка *(dams-kaya) su-machka*

hand luggage ручная кладь *ruch-na-ya klat'*

hand-made ручной работы *ruch-noi ra-bo-ti*

handicapped инвалид *inva-lit*

handkerchief носовой платок *nasa-voi pla-tok*

hangover похмелье *pa-khmyel-ye*

happen случаться *slu-chat-sa;* **what happened?** что случилось? *schto slu-chi-las'*

happy счастливый *shchis-li-vii*

harbour гавань *ga-van'*

hard твердый *tvyor-dii*

hat шляпа *schlya-pa*

have иметь *i-myet'*

hay fever сенная лихорадка *sin-na-ya likha-rat-ka*

hazelnut фундук *fun-duk*

he он *on*

head голова *gala-va*

headache головная боль *galav-na-ya bol'*

head waiter мэтрдотель *metrda-tel'*

hear слышать *sli-schat'*

heart сердце *syer-tse*

heart attack инфаркт *in-farkt*

heat жара *zha-ra*

heater обогреватель *abagri-va-tyel'*

heating отопление *ata-plye-niye*

heavy тяжелый *ti-zho-lii*

hello привет *pri-vyet;* (on telephone) алло *a-lo*

help[1] n помощь *po-mash;* **help!** помогите! *pama-gi-ti*

help[2] vb помогать *pama-gat;* **can you help me?** помогите мне пожалуйста? *pama-gi-ti mnye pa-zha-lusta*

herb трава *tra-va*

here здесь *zdyes'*

high высокий *vi-so-kii;* (number) большой *bal'-schoi*

high blood pressure высокое давление vi-**so**-kaye da-**vlye**-niye

high chair высокий детский стул vi-**so**-kii **dyet**-skii **stul**

high tide прилив pri-**lif**

hill холм **holm**

hire нанимать nani-**mat'**

hit ударить u-da-**rit'**

hitchhike путешествовать автостопом puti-**schest**-vavat' afta-**sto**-pam

hold держать dir-**zhat'**; (contain) содержать sadir-**zhat'**

hold-up (traffic jam) задержка za-**dyersch**-ka

hole дыра di-**ra**

holiday праздник **praz**-nik; on holiday в отпуске vot-**puskye**

home дом **dom**

homesick: to be homesick скучать по дому sku-**chat'** pa do-**mu**

honey мед **myot**

honeymoon медовый месяц mi-**do**-vii **mye**-sits

hope надежда na-**dyezh**-da; I hope so/not надеюсь, что да/нет na-**dye**-yus' schto **da/nyet**

hors d'oeuvre закуски za-**kus**-ki

horse лошадь **lo**-schat'

hospital больница bal'-**ni**-tsa

hot жаркий **zhar**-kii; (food) острый **os**-trii; I'm hot мне жарко **mnye zhar**-ka; it's too hot (food) это слишком остро e-ta **slisch**-kam **o**-stra; hot water горячая вода ga-**rya**-chaya va-**da**

hotel отель a-**tel'**

hour час **chas**; half an hour полчаса polchi-**sa**

house дом **dom**

house wine домашнее вино da-**masch**-niye vi-**no**

hovercraft судно на воздушной подушке **sud**-na na vaz-**dusch**-nai pa-**dusch**-ki

how (in what way) как **kak**; how much/many? сколько **skol'**-ka; how are you? как дела? **kak** di-**la**

hungry: I am hungry я хочу есть **ya** kha-**chu yest'**

hurry: I'm in a hurry я спешу **ya** spi-**schu**

hurt ушибить uschi-**bit'**; my back hurts у меня болит спина umi-**nya** ba-**lit** spi-**na**

husband муж **musch**

hydrofoil метеор; ракета miti-**or**; ra-**kye**-ta

I я **ya**

ice лед **lyot**

ice cream мороженое ma-**ro**-zhinaye

iced (drink) со льдом sa **l'dom**; (coffee, tea) холодный kha-**lod**-nii

ice lolly мороженое на палочке ma-**ro**-zhinaye na **pa**-lachki

ice rink каток ka-**tok**

if если **yes**-li

ignition зажигание zazhi-**ga**-niye

ill больной bal'-**noi**

immediately немедленно ni-**myed**-lina

important важный **vazh**-nii

impossible невозможно nivaz-**mozh**-na

in в **v**

inch see **CONVERSION CHARTS**

included включительно *fklyu-**chi**-til'na*

indigestion несварение желудка *nisva-**rye**-niye zhi-**lut**-ka*

indoors внутри помещения *vnu-**tri** pami-**shche**-niya; (at home)* дома *do-**ma***

infectious заразный *za-**raz**-nii*

information информация *infar-**ma**-tsiya*

information office бюро информации *byu-**ro** infar-**ma**-tsii*

injection укол *u-**kol***

injured пострадавший *pastra-**daf**-schii*

ink чернила *chir-**ni**-la*

insect насекомое *nasi-**ko**-maye*

insect bite укус насекомого *u-**kus** nasi-**ko**-mava*

insect repellent средство от насекомых *sryet-stva at nasi-**ko**-mikh*

inside внутри *vnu-**tri***

instant coffee растворимый кофе *rastva-**ri**-mii **ko**-fye*

instead вместо *vmyes-ta*

instructor инструктор *in-**struk**-tar*

insulin инсулин *insu-**lin***

insurance страховка *stra-**khof**-ka*

insurance certificate страховой полис *strakha-**voi** po-lis*

interesting интересный *inti-**ryes**-nii*

international интернациональный *internatsia-**nal'**-nii*

interpreter переводчик *piri-**vot**-chik*

into в *v*

invitation приглашение *prigla-**sche**-niye*

invite приглашать *prigla-**schat'***

invoice счет *shchot*

Ireland Ирландия *ir-**lan**-diya*

Irish *m/f/adj* ирландец/ирландка/ирландский *ir-**lan**-dits/ir-**lant**-ka/ir-**lan**-skii*

iron (for clothes)* утюг *u-**tyuk***

ironmonger's скобяные изделия *skabi-**ni**-ye iz-**dye**-liya*

is (to be) see **GRAMMAR**

island остров *ost-raf*

it оно *a-**no***

Italian *m/f/adj* итальянец/итальянка/итальянский *ital-ya-nits/ital-**yan**-ka/ital-**yans**-kii*

Italy Италия *i-**ta**-liya*

jacket пиджак *pid-**zhak***

jam (food)* варенье *va-**ryen'**-ye*

jammed заклинило *za-**kli**-nila*

jar (container)* банка *ban-ka*

jazz джаз *dzhaz*

jeans джинсы *dzhin-si*

jelly (dessert)* желе *zhe-**lye***

jellyfish мидуза *mi-**du**-za*

jersey джемпер *dzhem-pir*

jeweller's ювелирный магазин *yuvi-**lir**-nii maga-**zin***

jewellery драгоценности *draga-**tsen**-nasti*

Jewish еврейский *ye-**vrei**-skii*

job работа *ra-**bo**-ta*

jog: to go jogging бегать (трусцой) ***bye**-gat' (trus-tsoi)*

joke шутка *schut-ka*

journey путешествие *puti-schest-viye*

jug графин *gra-fin*

juice сок *sok*

jump leads соединительные провода для батареи *sayedi-ni-til'nii prava-da dlya bata-rye-i*

junction (road) железнодорожный узел *zhiliznada-rozh-nii u-zyel*

just: just me только я *tol'-ka ya*; **I've just arrived** я только что приехал(а) *ya tol'-ka schto pri-ye-khal(a)*

keep (retain) хранить *khra-nit'*

kettle чайник *chai-nik*

key ключ *klyuch*

kidneys почки *poch-ki*

kilo кило(грамм) *kila-gram*

kilometre километр *kila-myetr*

kind[1] *n* (sort, type) вид *vit*

kind[2] *adj* (person) добрый *do-brii*

kiss[1] *n* поцелуй *patsi-lui*

kiss[2] *vb* целовать *tsila-vat'*

kitchen кухня *kukh-nya*

knife нож *nosch*

know знать *znat'*; **I don't know** я не знаю *ya ni zna-yu*

lace (fabric) кружева *kruzhi-va*

ladder лестница *lyes'-nitsa*

Ladies' женский туалет *zhen-skii tua-lyet*

lady дама *da-ma*

lager (светлое) пиво *(svyet-laye) pi-va*

lake озеро *o-zira*

lamb (meat) баранина *ba-ra-nina*

lamp лампа *lam-pa*

lane линия *li-niya*; (of motorway) полоса *pala-sa*

language язык *ya-zik*

large большой *bal'-schoi*

last последний *pa-slyed-nii*; **last week** на прошлой неделе *na prosch-lai ni-dye-lye*

late поздний *poz-nii*; **the train is late** поезд опаздывает *po-ist a-paz-divait*; **sorry we are late** извините за опоздание *izvi-ni-tye za apaz-da-niye*

later позже *po-zhe*

Launderette прачечная *pra-chischnaya*

laundry service стирка белья *stir-ka bil'-ya*

lavatory туалет *tua-lyet*

lawyer юрист *yu-rist*

laxative слабительное *sla-bi-til'naye*

layby обочина *a-bo-china*

lead *n* (electric) провод *pro-vat*

leader лидер *li-dyer*; (guide) гид *git*

leak (of gas, liquid) утечка *u-tyech-ka*; (in roof) протечка *pra-tyech-ka*

learn учить *u-chit'*

least: at least по крайней мере *pa krai-nii mye-rye*

leather кожа *ko-zha*

leave (depart) уезжать *uye-zhat'*; **when does the train leave?** когда отходит поезд? *kag-da at-kho-dit po-ist*

leek порей *pa-ryei*

left: on the left слева *slye-va*; **to the**

left налево *na-lye-va*

left luggage камера хранения *ka-mira khra-nye-niya*

leg нога *na-ga*

lemon лимон *li-mon*

lemonade лимонад *lima-nat*

lemon tea чай с лимоном *chai slimo-nam*

lend давать взаймы *da-vat' vzai-mi*

Leningrad see St Petersburg

lens линза *lin-za*

less меньше *myen'-sche*

lesson урок *u-rok*

let (allow) разрешать *razri-schat'* ; (hire out) сдавать *zda-vat'*

letter письмо *pis'-mo*

lettuce салат *sa-lat*

library библиотека *biblia-tye-ka*

licence (driving) (водительские) права *(va-di-til'skii) pra-va*

lid крышка *krisch-ka*

lie down прилечь *pri-lyech*

lifeboat спасательная шлюпка *spa-sa-til'naya schlyup-ka*

lifeguard спасатель *spa-sa-til'*

life jacket спасательный жилет *spa-sa-til'nii zhi-lyet*

lift лифт *lift*; (ski) подъемник *pad-yom-nik*

light свет *svuet*; **have you got a light?** у вас есть спички? *u vas yest' spich-ki*

light bulb лампочка *lam-pachka*

lighter зажигалка *zazhi-gal-ka*

like¹ prep как *kak;* **like you** как вы *kak vi;* **like this** как это *kak e-ta*

like² vb любить *lyu-bit';* **I like coffee** мне нравится кофе *mnye*

nra-vitsa ko-fye; **I would like a newspaper** мне нужна газета *mnye nuzh-na ga-zye-ta*

line (row, phone) линия *li-niya*

lip salve гигиеническая помада *gigiye-ni-chiskaya pa-ma-da*

lipstick губная помада *gub-na-ya pa-ma-da*

liqueur ликер *li-kyor*

listen (to) слушать *slu-schat'*

litre литр *litr*

little: a little milk немного молока *ni-mno-ga mala-ka*

live жить *zhit';* **I live in London** я живу в Лондоне *ya zhi-vu vlon-dani*

liver печень *pye-chin'*

living room гостиная *gas-ti-naya*

loaf буханка *bu-khan-ka*

lobster омар *a-mar*

local (wine, speciality) местный *myes-nii*

lock¹ vb (door) закрывать *zakri-vat'*

lock² n (on door, box) замок *za-mok*

lollipop леденец (на палочке) *lidi-nyets (na pa-lachki)*

London Лондон *lon-dan*

long длинный *dli-nii;* **for a long time** долго *dol-ga*

look смотреть *sma-tryet';* (seem) казаться *ka-za-tsa;* **to look after** присматривать за *pri-smat-rivat' za;* **to look for** искать *is-kat'*

lorry грузовик *gruza-vik*

lose терять *ti-ryat'*

lost (object) потерянный *pa-tye-ryanii;* **I have lost my wallet** я потерял(а) кошелек *ya pati-ryal(a)* *kaschi-lyok;* I am lost я потерялся (потерялась) *ya pati-ryal-sya (pati-rya-las')*

lost property office бюро находок *byu-ro na-kho-dak*

lot: a lot много *mno-ga*

lotion лосьон *la-syon*

loud громкий *grom-kii*

lounge *(airport)* зал ожидания *zal azhi-da-niya; (at home)* гостиная *gas-ti-naya*

love *vb* любить *lyu-bit';* I love swimming я люблю плавать *ya lyu-blyu pla-vat'*

lovely милый *mi-lii*

low низкий *nis-kii*

low tide отлив *at-lif*

lucky счастливый *shchis-li-vii*

luggage багаж *ba-gasch*

luggage allowance норма провоза багажа *nor-ma pra-vo-za baga-zha*

luggage rack *(on car, in train)* багажная полка *ba-gazh-naya pol-ka*

luggage tag багажная этикетка *ba-gazh-naya eti-kyet-ka*

luggage trolley багажная тележка *ba-gazh-naya ti-lyesch-ka*

lunch обед *a-byet*

luxury роскошный *ras-kosch-nii*

machine машина *ma-schi-na*

madam мадам *ma-dam*

magazine журнал *zhur-nal*

maid *(in hotel)* горничная *gor-nichnaya*

main главный *glav-nii*

main course второе блюдо *fta-ro-ye blyu-da*

mains *(electric)* сеть *syet'*

make¹ *vb* делать *dye-lat'*

make² *n (brand)* марка *mar-ka*

make-up макияж *maki-yasch*

man мужчина *mu-shchi-na*

manager менеджер *me-nidzher*

many много *mno-ga*

map карта *kar-ta*

margarine маргарин *marga-rin*

mark *(stain)* пятно *pit-no*

market рынок *ri-nak*

marmalade апельсиновый джем *apil'-si-navii dzhem*

married *(man)* женатый *zhi-na-tii; (woman)* замужняя *za-muzh-nyaya*

marrow *(vegetable)* кабачок *kaba-chok*

marzipan марципан *martsi-pan*

mascara тушь для ресниц *tusch dlya ris-nits*

mass *(in church)* месса *myes-sa*

matches спички *spich-ki*

material *(cloth)* материя *ma-tye-riya*

matter: it doesn't matter это не важно *e-ta ni vazh-na;* what's the matter? что случилось? *schto slu-chi-las'*

mayonnaise майонез *maya-nes*

meal еда *ye-da*

mean *(signify)* значить *zna-chit';* what does this mean? что это значит? *schto e-ta zna-chit*

meat мясо *mya-sa*

mechanic механик *mi-kha-nik*

medicine лекарство *li-kar-stva*

medium (size) средний *sryed*-nii; (medium sweet champagne) полусладкое *polu-slat*-kaye

medium rare средней зажаренности *sryed*-nii za-*zha*-rinasti

meet встречать *fstri-chat'*

melon дыня *di*-nya

melt таять *ta*-yat'

member (of club, etc) член *chlyen*

men мужчины mu-*shchi*-ni

menu меню mi-*nyu*

meringue безе bi-*ze*

message (on paper) записка za-*pis*-ka

meter счетчик *shchot*-chik

metre метр *myetr*

migraine мигрень mi-*gryen'*

milk молоко mala-*ko*

milkshake молочный коктейль ma-*loch*-nii kak-*tel'*

millimetre миллиметр mili-*myetr*

million миллион mili-*on*

mind: do you mind if I...? вы не против если я...? *vi ni pro*-tiv *yes*-li *ya*...

mineral water минеральная вода mini-*ral'*-naya va-*da*

minimum минимум *mi*-nimum

minor road небольшая дорога nibal'-*scha*-ya da-ro-ga

mint (herb) мята *mya*-ta; (sweets) ментоловый леденец min-*to*-lavii lidi-*nyets*

minute минута mi-*nu*-ta

mirror зеркало *zyer*-kala

miss (train, etc) упустить upu-*stit'*

missing: my son is missing мой сын пропал *moi sin* pra-*pal*

mistake ошибка a-*schip*-ka

misty туманный tu-*man*-nii

misunderstanding: there's been a misunderstanding это недоразумение *e*-ta nidarazu-*mye*-niye

modern современный savri-*myen*-nii

moisturizer увлажнитель uvlazh-*ni*-til'

monastery монастырь manas-*tir'*

money деньги *dyen'*-gi

money order денежный перевод *dye*-nizhnii piri-*vot*

month месяц *mye*-sits

more: more than 3 больше трех *bol'*-sche *tryokh*; **more vodka, please** еще водки, пожалуйста ye-*shcho vot*-ki pa-*zha*-lusta

morning утро *u*-tra

Moscow Москва mas-*kva*

mosquito комар ka-*mar*

mother мама *ma*-ma

motor мотор ma-*tor*

motor boat моторная лодка ma-*tor*-naya *lot*-ka

motorcycle мотоцикл mata-*tsikl*

motorway автострада afta-*stra*-da

mountain гора ga-*ra*

mouth рот *rot*

move: it isn't moving он(а) не движется *on*(a) ni *dvi*-zhitsa

much: it costs too much это слишком дорого *e*-ta *slisch*-kam *do*-raga

museum музей mu-*zyei*

mushroom гриб *grip*; to pick

mushrooms собирать грибы *sabirat' gri-bi*

music музыка *mu-zika*

mussel мидия *mi-diya*

must должен *dol-zhin*

mustard горчица *gar-chi-tsa*

mutton баранина *ba-ra-nina*

nail (metal) гвоздь *gvost'*

nail polish лак для ногтей *lak dlya nak-tyei*

naked голый *go-lii*

name имя *i-mya*

napkin салфетка *sal-fyet-ka*

nappy пеленка *pi-lyon-ka*

narrow узкий *us-kii*

nationality национальность *natsianal'-nast'*

navy blue темно-синий *tyom-na-si-nii*

near: is it near? это близко? *e-ta blis-ka*

necessary необходимо *niapkha-di-ma*

neck шея *sche-ya*

necklace ожерелье *azhi-ryel-ye*

need: I need an aspirin мне нужен аспирин *mnye nu-zhin aspi-rin*

needle игла *i-gla*; **a needle and thread** иголка с ниткой *i-gol-ka snit-kai*

negative (photography) негатив *niga-tif*

neighbour m/f сосед/ка *sa-syet/ka*

nerves нервы *nyer-vi*

never никогда *nikag-da*; **I never drink wine** я никогда не пью вина *ya nikag-da ni pyu vi-na*

new новый *no-vii*

news новости *no-vasti*

newsagent газетный киоск *ga-zyet-nii ki-osk*

newspaper газета *ga-zye-ta*

New Year Новый Год *no-vii got*

New Zealand Новая Зеландия *no-vaya zi-lan-diya*

next: the next stop следующая остановка *slye-dushchaya asta-nof-ka*; **next week** на следующей неделе *na slye-dushchei ni-dye-lye*

nice приятный *pri-yat-nii*

night ночь *noch*; **at night** ночью *no-chyu*

night club ночной клуб *na-chnoi klup*

nightdress ночная рубашка *na-chna-ya ru-basch-ka*

no нет *nyet*; **no, thank you** спасибо, не надо *spa-si-ba ni na-da*

nobody никто *ni-kto*

noisy шумный *schum-nii*

nonalcoholic безалкогольный *bizalka-gol'-nii*

none: there's none left все кончилось *fsyo kon-chilas'*

nonsmoking (compartment) для некурящих *dlya niku-rya-shchikh*

north север *sye-vir*

Northern Ireland Северная Ирландия *sye-virnaya ir-lan-diya*

not: I don't know я не знаю *ya ni zna-yu*

note записка *za-pis-ka*

note pad блокнот *blak-not*

nothing ничего *nichi-vo*

now сейчас *si-chas*

number номер *no-mir*

nurse медсестра *myetsi-stra*

nursery slope трасса для новичков *tra-sa dlya navich-kof*

nut (peanut) арахис *a-ra-khis*; (walnut) грецкий орех *gryets-kii a-ryekh*; (hazelnut) фундук *fun-duk*

occasionally иногда *inag-da*

off: turn it off! выключите! *vi-klyuchiti*; **this meat is off** это несвежее мясо *e-ta ni-svye-zhiye mya-sa*

offer предложение *pridla-zhe-niye*

office офис *o-fis*

often часто *chas-ta*

oil масло *mas-la*

oil filter масляный фильтр *mas-lyanii fil'tr*

ointment мазь *mas'*

OK окей *o-kyei*

old старый *sta-rii*; **how old are you?** сколько вам лет? *skol'-ka vam lyet*

olive oil оливковое масло *a-lif-kavaye mas-la*

olives оливки *a-lif-ki*

omelette омлет *am-lyet*

on: on the table на столе *nasta-lye*

once однажды *ad-nazh-di*

one *m/f/nt* один/одна/одно *a-din/a-dna/a-dno*

one-way street (street) улица с односторонним движением *u-litsa sadnasta-ron-im dvi-zhe-niyem*; **one-way** (ticket) билет в один конец *bi-lyet va-din ka-nyets*

onion лук *luk*

only только *tol'-ka*

open¹ adj открытый *at-kri-tii*

open² vb открывать *atkri-vat'*

opera опера *o-pira*

operator оператор *api-ra-tar*

opposite напротив *na-pro-tif*; **opposite the hotel** напротив гостиницы *na-pro-tif gas-ti-nitsi*

or или *i-li*

orange¹ adj (colour) оранжевый *a-ran-zhivii*

orange² n апельсин *apil'-sin*

orange juice апельсиновый сок *apil'-si-navii sok*

order vb заказать *zaka-zat'*

original настоящий *nasta-ya-shchii*

other: the other one другой *dru-goi*; **do you have any others?** у вас есть другие? *u vas yest' dru-gi-ye*

ounce унция *un-tsiya* see **CONVERSION CHARTS**

out: he's out его нет *ye-vo nyet*

outdoors (pool, etc) на открытом воздухе *naat-kri-tam voz-dukhe*

outside снаружи *sna-ru-zhi*

oven духовка *du-khof-ka*

over: over there там *tam*

overcharge (money) обсчитывать *ap-shchi-tivat'*

overnight (travel) ночной *nach-noi*

owe: I owe you… я буду вам должен… *ya bu-du vam dol-zhin*

owner хозяин *kha-zya-in*

oysters устрицы *u-stritsi*

pack (luggage) паковать *paka-vat'*

package пакет *pa-kyet*

package tour комплексный тур *kom-plyeksnii tur*

packed lunch сухой паек *su-khoi pa-yok*

packet пачка *pach-ka*

paid оплаченный *a-pla-chinii*

painful больной *bal'-noi*

painkiller болеутоляющее (средство) *bolyeuta-lya-yushcheye (sryet-stva)*

painter художник *khu-dozh-nik*

painting картина *kar-ti-na*

pair пара *pa-ra*

palace дворец *dva-ryets*

pan кастрюля *kas-tryu-lya*

pancakes блины *bli-ni*

panties трусики *tru-siki*

pants штаны *schta-ni*

paper бумага *bu-ma-ga*

paraffin парафин *para-fin*

parcel посылка *pa-sil-ka*

pardon *(I didn't understand)* простите? *pras-ti-ti;* **I beg your pardon!** прошу прощения! *pra-schu pra-shchye-niya*

parents родители *ra-di-tili*

park[1] *n* парк *park*

park[2] *vb* парковать *parka-vat'*

parsley петрушка *pi-trusch-ka*

part часть *chast'*

party *(group)* партия *par-tiya;* *(evening)* вечер *vye-chir*

passenger пасажир *pasa-zhir*

passport паспорт *pas-part*

passport control паспортный контроль *pas-partnii kan-trol'*

pasta паста *pas-ta*

pastry выпечка *vi-pyechka*

pâté паштет *pasch-tyet*

path тропа *tra-pa*

pay платить *pla-tit'*

payment плата *pla-ta*

peace мир *mir;* **war and peace** война и мир *vai-na i mir*

peach персик *pyer-sik*

peanut арахис *a-ra-khis*

pear груша *gru-scha*

peas горох *ga-rokh*

peel *(fruit)* чистить *chis-tit'*

peg *(for clothes)* вешалка *vye-schalka;* *(for tent)* колышек *ko-lischik*

pen ручка *ruch-ka*

pencil карандаш *karan-dasch*

penicillin пенициллин *pinitsi-lin*

penknife перочинный нож *pira-chi-nii nosch*

pensioner пенсионер *pyensia-nyer*

pepper перец *pye-rits*

per в *v;* **per hour** в час *fchas;* **per week** в неделю *vni-dye-lyu*

perfect отличный *a-tlich-nii*

performance представление *pritstav-lye-niye*

perfume духи *du-khi*

perhaps может быть *mo-zhit bit'*

period *(menstruation)* менструации *myenstru-a-tsii*

perm перманент *pirma-nyent*

permit разрешение *razri-sche-niye*

person человек *chila-vyek*

petrol бензин *bin-zin*

petrol station бензоколонка *binzaka-lon-ka*

phone *see* **telephone**

photocopy *n* фотокопия *fata-ko-piya*

photograph n фотография *fata-gra-fiya*

picnic пикник *pik-nik*

picture (painting) картина *kar-ti-na*

pie пирог *pi-rok*

piece кусок *ku-sok*

pill таблетка *ta-blyet-ka*

pillow подушка *pa-dusch-ka*

pillowcase наволочка *na-valachka*

pin (hair) заколка *za-kol-ka*

pineapple ананас *ana-nas*

pink розовый *ro-zavii*

pint: a pint of beer кружка пива *krusch-ka pi-va*

pipe труба *tru-ba*

plane самолет *sama-lyot*

plaster (sticking plaster) пластырь *plas-tir'*; (for broken limbs) гипс *gips*

plastic пластик *plas-tik*

plate тарелка *ta-ryel-ka*

platform платформа *plat-for-ma*

play играть *i-grat'*

playroom игровая комната *igra-va-ya kom-nata*

please пожалуйста *pa-zha-lusta*

pleased довольный *da-vol'-nii*

plug (electrical) штепсель *schtep-sil'*; (for sink) пробка *prop-ka*

plum слива *sli-va*

plumber сантехник *san-tyekh-nik*

points (in car) контакты *kan-tak-ti*

police милиция *mi-li-tsiya*

policeman милиционер *militsia-nyer*

police station отделение милиции *atdi-lye-niye mi-li-tsii*

polish (for shoes) крем для обуви *kryem dlya o-buvi*

polluted загрязненный *zagryaz-nyo-nii*

pool (swimming) бассейн *ba-sein*

popular популярный *papu-lyar-nii*

pork свинина *svi-ni-na*

port (harbour) порт *port*

porter насильщик *na-sil'-shchik*

possible возможный *vaz-mozh-nii*

post[1] n (letters) почта *poch-ta*

post[2] vb отправлять *atprav-lyat'*

postbox почтовый ящик *pach-to-vii ya-shchik*

postcard открытка *at-krit-ka*

postcode (почтовый) индекс (*pach-to-vii*) *in-deks*

post office почта *poch-ta*

pot (for cooking) горшок *gar-schok*

potato картофель *kar-to-fil'*

pottery керамика *ki-ra-mika*

pound (weight, money) фунт *funt*

pram коляска *ka-lyas-ka*

prawns креветки *kri-vyet-ki*

prefer предпочитать *pryetpachi-tat'*

pregnant беременная *bi-rye-minaya*

prepare готовить *ga-to-vit'*

prescription рецепт *ri-tsept*

present (gift) подарок *pa-da-rak*

pretty милый *mi-lii*

price цена *tsi-na*

priest священник *svi-shchen-nik*

print (photo) печатать *pi-cha-tat'*

private частный *chas-nii*

probably вероятно *vira-yat-na*

problem проблема *prab-lye-ma*

programme программа *pra-gra-ma*

pronounce: how do you pronounce this? как это произносится? *kak e-ta praiz-no-sitsa*

Protestant *adj* протестантский *pratis-tan-skii*

prune чернослив *chirna-slif*

public общественный *ap-shchest-vinii*

public holiday всеобщий праздник *fsye-op-shchii praz-nik*

pudding пудинг *pu-dink*

pull тянуть *ti-nut'*

pullover пуловер *pu-lo-vyer*

puncture прокол *pra-kol*

purple лиловый *li-lo-vii*

purse кошелек *kaschi-lyok*

push толкать *tal-kat'*; *(sign on door)* от себя *atsi-bya*

put *(insert)* вставлять *fstav-lyat'*; *(put down)* класть *klast'*

pyjamas пижама *pi-zha-ma*

queue *n* очередь *o-chirit'*

quick быстрый *bi-strii*

quickly быстро *bi-stra*

quiet *(place)* тихий *ti-khii*

quilt стеганое одеяло *styo-ganaye adi-ya-la*

quite: it's quite good довольно хороший *da-vol'-na kha-ro-schii*; **it's quite expensive** довольно дорого *da-vol'-na do-raga*

racket ракетка *ra-kyet-ka*

radio радио *ra-dio*

radish редис *rye-dis*

railway station вокзал *vak-zal*

rain дождь *doscht'*

raincoat плащ *plash*

raining: it's raining идет дождь *i-dyot doscht'*

raisin изюм *i-zyum*

rare *(unique)* редкий *ryet-kii*; *(steak)* с кровью *skrov-yu*

raspberry малина *ma-li-na*

rate: rate of exchange курс *kurs*

raw сырой *si-roi*

razor бритва *brit-va*

razor blades лезвия для бритвы *lyez-viya dlya brit-vi*

ready готовый *ga-to-vii*

real настоящий *nasta-ya-shchii*

receipt чек *chyek*

recently недавно *ni-dav-na*

reception (desk) прием (гостей) *pri-yom (gas-tyei)*

recipe рецепт *ri-tsept*

recommend рекомендовать *rikaminda-vat'*

record *(music, etc)* запись *za-pis'*

red красный *kras-nii*

reduction снижение *sni-zhe-niye*

refill *(pen, lighter, etc)* заправка *za-praf-ka*

refund компенсация *kampin-sa-tsiya*

registered *(letter)* заказное *zakaz-no-ye*

regulations правила *pra-vila*

reimburse возмещать *vazmi-shchat'*

relation *(family)* родственник *rot-stvinik*

relax отдыхать *atdi-khat'*

reliable *(company, service)* надежный *na-dyozh-nii*

remain оставаться *asta-vat-sa*

remember помнить ***pom**-nit'*

rent *(house, car)* нанимать *nani-**mat**'*

rental *(house, car)* плата ***pla**-ta*

repair *n* ремонт *ri-**mont***

repeat повторять *pafta-**ryat**'*

reservation резервирование *ryezyer-**vi**-ravaniye*

reserve заказать заранее *zaka-**zat**' za-ra-niye*

reserved заказано *za-ka-zana*

rest[1] *n (remainder)* остаток *as-ta-tak;* **the rest of the wine** оставшееся вино *as-taf-scheyesya vi-**no***

rest[2] *vb* отдыхать *atdi-**khat**'*

restaurant ресторан *rista-**ran***

restaurant car вагон-ресторан *va-gon rista-**ran***

return *(go back)* возвращаться *vazvra-**shchat**-sa; (give back)* отдавать *atda-**vat**'*

return ticket билет в оба конца *bi-**lyet** vo-ba kan-tsa*

reverse charge call с оплатой на другом конце *sa-**pla**-tai nadru-**gom** kan-tse*

rheumatism ревматизм *rivma-**tizm***

rhubarb ревень *ri-**vyen**'*

rice рис *ris*

riding: to go riding ездить верхом *yez-dit' vir-**khom***

right[1] *adj (correct)* правильный ***pra**-vil'nii*

right[2] *: on the right* справа *spra-va;* **to the right** направо *na-**pra**-va*

ring кольцо *kal'-**tso***

ripe зрелый ***zrye**-lii*

river река *ri-**ka***

road дорога *da-**ro**-ga*

road map атлас дорог ***at**-las da-**rok***

roast жареный ***zha**-rinii*

roll *(bread)* рулет *ru-**lyet***

roof крыша ***kri**-scha*

room *(in hotel)* номер ***no**-mir; (in house)* комната ***kom**-nata;* **is there enough room for us?** на нас есть место *na nas yest' **myes**-ta*

room service обслуживание в номере *ap-**slu**-zhivaniye **vno**-mirye*

rope веревка *vi-**ryof**-ka*

rosé розовый *ro-**zavii***

rough *(sea)* неспокойный *nispa-**koi**-nii*

round круглый ***krug**-lii;* **round the world** вокруг света *va-**kruk** svye-ta*

route маршрут *mar-**schrut***

rowing boat гребная лодка *gryeb-na-ya **lot**-ka*

rubber резина *ri-**zi**-na*

rubber band резинка *ri-**zin**-ka*

rubbish мусор ***mu**-sar*

rucksack рюкзак *ryuk-**zak***

ruins развалины *raz-va-lini*

rum ром *rom*

rush hour час пик *chas **pik***

Russian[1] *m/f/adj* русский/ русская/русский *rus-kii/rus-kaya/rus-kii*

Russian[2] **: I don't speak Russian** я не говорю по-русски *ya ni gava-**ryu** pa-**rus**-ki*

safe[1] *n* сейф ***seif***

safe[2] *adj (beach, medicine)* безопасный *biza-**pas**-nii*

safety pin (английская) булавка (an-**gli**-skaya) bu-**laf**-ka

sail парус pa-rus

sailing (sport) плавание под парусом pla-vanye pat pa-rusam

St Petersburg Санкт-Петербург sant-pitir-burk

salad салат sa-lat

salad dressing приправа к салату pri-**pra**-va ksa-la-tu

salmon лосось la-sos'

salt соль sol'

same: I'll have the same мне то же самое mnye to zhe sa-maye

sand песок pi-sok

sandals сандали san-da-li

sandwich бутерброд buter-**brot**

sanitary towel гигиеническая прокладка gigiye-**ni**-chiskaya pra-**klat**-ka

sardine сардина sar-**di**-na

sauce соус so-us

saucepan кастрюля kas-**tryu**-lya

saucer соусник so-usnik

sauna сауна sa-una

sausage колбаса kalba-sa

savoury (not sweet) остро-соленый ostra-sa-**lyo**-nii

say говорить gava-**rit'**

scallop эскалоп eska-**lop**

scarf (long) шарф scharf; (headscarf) платок pla-**tok**

school школа schko-la

scissors ножницы nozh-nitzi

Scotland Шотландия schat-lan-diya

Scottish m/f/adj шотландец/ шотландка/шотландский schat-lan-dits/schat-**lant**-ka/shat-**lan**-skii

screw винт vint

screwdriver отвертка at-**vyort**-ka

sculpture (object) скульптура skul'p-**tu**-ra

sea море mo-rye

seafood морепродукты moryepra-**duk**-ti

seasickness морская болезнь mars-ka-ya ba-**lyezn'**

seaside: at the seaside на море na mo-rye

season ticket проездной билет на сезон prayez-**noi** bi-**lyet** nasi-**zon**

seat (chair, train, etc) место myes-ta

second второй fta-roi

second-class ticket билет второго класса bi-**lyet** fta-ro-va kla-sa

see видеть vi-**dyet'**

self-service самообслуживание samaap-**slu**-zhivaniye

sell продавать prada-**vat'**

sellotape скотч skoch

send посылать pasi-**lat'**

senior citizens старшее поколение star-scheye paka-**lye**-niye

separate отдельный at-**dyel'**-nii

serious серьезный sir-**yoz**-nii

serve служить slu-**zhit'**

service (in restaurant) обслуживание ap-**slu**-zhivaniye

service charge наценка за обслуживание na-**tsen**-ka zaap-**slu**-zhivaniye

set menu комплексное меню kom-pliksnaye mi-**nyu**

shade тень tyen'

shallow мелкий *myel*-kii

shampoo шампунь *scham-pun'*

shampoo and set помыть и уложить *pa-mit' iula-zhit'*

share делить *di-lit'*

shave брить *brit'*

shaving cream крем для бритья *kryem dlya bri-tya*

she она *a-na*

sheet простыня *prasti-nya*

shellfish ракушки *ra-kusch-ki*

sherry херес *khye-ris*

ship корабль *ka-rabl'*

shirt рубашка *ru-basch-ka*

shock absorber амортизатор *amarti-za-tar*

shoes туфли *tuf-li*

shop магазин *maga-zin*

shopping: to go shopping ходить по магазинам *kha-dit' pamaga-zi-nam*

short короткий *ka-rot-kii*

short-cut короткий путь *ka-rot-kii put'*

shorts шорты *schor-ti*

show¹ *n* представление *pritstav-lye-niye*

show² *vb* показывать *pa-ka-zivat'*

shower душ *dusch*

sick *(ill)* больной *bal'-noi*

sightseeing tour обзорная экскурсия *ab-zor-naya iks-kur-siya*

sign знак *znak*

signature подпись *pot-pis'*

silk шелк *scholk*

silver серебро *siri-bro*

similar похожий *pa-kho-zhii*

simple простой *pras-toi*

single *(unmarried)* холостой *khalas-toi*; *(not double)* одиночный *adi-noch-nii*

single bed односпальная кровать *adna-spal'-naya kra-vat'*

single room комната на одного *kom-nata naadna-vo*

sink раковина *ra-kavina*

sir сэр *ser*

sister сестра *sis-tra*

sit сидеть *si-dyet'*

size размер *raz-myer*

skates коньки *kan'-ki*

skating катание на коньках *ka-ta-niye nakan'-kakh*

skin кожа *ko-zha*

skirt юбка *yup-ka*

sleep спать *spat'*

sleeper *(in train)* спальный вагон *spal'-nii va-gon*

sleeping bag спальный мешок *spal'-nii mi-schok*

sleeping car спальный вагон *spal'-nii va-gon*

sleeping pill снотворное *sna-tvor-naye*

slice кусок *ku-sok*

slide *(photograph)* слайд *slaid*

slippers тапочки *ta-pachki*

slow медленный *mye-dlinii*

small маленький *ma-lin'kii*

smaller меньше *myen'-sche*

smell¹ *n (pleasant)* запах *za-pakh*

smell² *vb* пахнуть *pakh-nut'*

smoke¹ *n* дым *dim*

smoke² *vb* курить *ku-rit'*

smoked копченый *kap-cho-nii*

snack bar закусочная *za-ku-sachnaya*

snorkel трубка акваланга *trup-ka akva-lan-ga*

snow снег *snyek*

snowed up заснеженый *za-snye-zhinii*

snowing: it's snowing идет снег *i-dyot snyek*

so: so much так много *tak mno-ga*

soap мыло *mi-lo*

soap powder стиральный порошок *sti-ral'-nii para-schok*

sober трезвый *tryez-vii*

sock носок *na-sok*

socket (electric) розетка *ra-zyet-ka*

soda сода *so-da*

soft мягкий *myakh-kii*

soft drink безалкогольный напиток *bizalka-gol'-nii na-pi-tak*

someone кто-нибудь *kto-nibut'*

something что-нибудь *schto-nibut'*

sometimes иногда *inag-da*

son сын *sin*

song песня *pyes-nya*

soon скоро *sko-ra*; **as soon as possible** как можно скорее *kak mozh-na ska-rye-ye*

sore: I've got a sore throat у меня болит горло *umi-nya ba-lit gor-la*

sorry: I'm sorry! (apology) извините! *izvi-ni-ti*; **I'm sorry** (regret) жалко! *zhal-ka*

sort: what sort of cheese? какой это сыр? *ka-koi e-ta sir*

soup суп *sup*

south юг *yuk*

souvenir сувенир *suvi-nir*

space: parking space место для парковки *myes-ta dlya par-kof-ki*

spade лопата *la-pa-ta*

spanner гаечный ключ *ga-yechnii klyuch*

spare wheel запасное колесо *zapas-no-ye kali-so*

spark plug зажигание *zazhi-ga-niye*

sparkling (wine) игристое *i-gris-taye*

speak говорить *gava-rit'*

special особый *a-so-bii*

speciality (restaurant) фирменное блюдо *fir-minaye blyu-da*

speed скорость *sko-rast'*

speed limit максимальная скорость *maksi-mal'-naya sko-rast'*

spell: how do you spell it? как это пишется? *kak e-ta pi-schitsa*

spicy острый *os-trii*

spinach шпинат *schpi-nat*

spirits крепкие напитки *kryep-kii na-pit-ki*

sponge губка *gup-ka*

spoon ложка *losch-ka*

sport спорт *sport*

spring (season) весна *vis-na*

square (in town) площадь *plo-shchat'*

stairs ступеньки *stu-pyen'-ki*

stalls (theatre) ложи *lo-zhi*

stamp марка *mar-ka*

start начинать *nachi-nat'*

starter (in meal) закуски *za-kus-ki*; (in car) стартер *star-tyor*

station станция *stan-tsiya*

stationer's канцелярские товары

kantsi-**lyars**-kii ta-**va**-ri

stay (remain) оставаться asta-**vat**-sa;
I'm staying at a hotel я
остановился(лась) в гостинице
ya astana-**vi**-lsya(las') vgas-**ti**-nitsye

steak антрекот antri-**kot**

steep крутой kru-**toi**

sterling фунт стерлингов **funt
styer**-lingaf

stew тушеное блюдо tu-**scho**-naye
blyu-da

steward стюарт styu-**art**

stewardess стюардесса styuar-
de-sa

sticking plaster пластырь **plas**-tir'

still (motionless) неподвижный
nipa-**dvizh**-nii

sting жалить zha-**lit**'

stockings чулки chul-**ki**

stomach живот zhi-**vot**

stomach upset расстроенный
желудок ras-**tro**-inii zhi-**lu**-dak

stop стоп **stop**

stopover остановка asta-**nof**-ka

storm буря **bu**-rya

straight on прямо **prya**-ma

straw (for drinking) соломинка sa-
lo-minka

strawberry клубника klub-**ni**-ka

street улица **u**-litsa

street map план города **plan** go-
rada

string бичевка bi-**chof**-ka

striped в полоску fpa-**los**-ku

strong сильный sil'-**nii**

stuck застрять za-**stryat**'

student студент stu-**dyent**

stung быть ужаленным **bit**' u-zha-
linim

stupid глупый **glu**-pii

suddenly вдруг **vdruk**

suede замша **zam**-scha

sugar сахар sa-**khar**

suit костюм kas'-**tyum**

suitcase чемодан chima-**dan**

summer лето **lye**-ta

sun солнце **son**-tse

sunbathe загарать zaga-**rat**'

sun block лосьон от загара **las**'-
yon at za-**ga**-ra

sunburn n сгорать zga-**rat**'

sunglasses солнечные очки **sol**-
nichniye ach-**ki**

sunny солнечно **sol**-nichna; **it's
sunny** светит солнце **svye**-tit
son-tse

sunshade тень **tyen**'

sunstroke солнечный удар **sol**-
nichnii u-**dar**

supermarket универсам univir-**sam**

supper (dinner) ужин **u**-zhin

supplement дополнение dapal-**nye**-
niye

sure уверенный u-**vye**-rinii

surfboard доска для серфинга
das-**ka** dlya **ser**-finga

surfing серфинг **ser**-fink

surname фамилия fa-**mi**-liya

suspension рессоры ris-**so**-ri

sweater свитер **svi**-ter

sweet сладкий **slat**-kii

sweets сласти **slas**-ti

swim плавать **pla**-vat'

swimming pool бассейн ba-**sein**

swimsuit купальник *ku-pal'-nik*

Swiss *m/f/adj* швейцарец/ швейцарка/швейцарский *schvi-tsa-rits/schvi-tsar-ka/schvi-tsars-kii*

switch выключатель *viklu-cha-til'*

switch off выключать *viklyu-chat'*

switch on включать *fklyu-chat'*

Switzerland Швейцария *schvei-tsa-riya*

synagogue синагога *sina-go-ga*

t-shirt футболка *fut-bol-ka*

tablecloth скатерть *ska-tirt'*

tablespoon столовая ложка *sta-lo-vaya losch-ka*

tablet таблетка *tab-lyet-ka*

table tennis настольный теннис *na-stol'-nii te-nis*

take *(carry)* брать *brat'* ; *(grab)* хватать *khva-tat'* ; **how long does it take?** сколько на это нужно времени? *skol'-ka na e-ta nuzh-na vrye-mini*

talc тальк *tal'k*

talk разговаривать *razga-va-rivat'*

tall высокий *vi-so-kii*

tampons тампоны *tam-po-ni*

tap кран *kran*

tape лента *lyen-ta*

tape-recorder магнитофон *magnita-fon*

taste[1] *vb* : **can I taste some?** можно попробовать? *mozh-na pa-pro-bavat'*

taste[2] *n* вкус *fkus*

tax налог *na-lok*

taxi такси *ta-ksi*

taxi rank стоянка такси *sta-yan-ka ta-ksi*

tea чай *chai*

teabag чайный пакетик *chai-nii pa-kye-tik*

teach учить *u-chit'*

teacher учитель *u-chi-til'*

teapot заварочный чайник *za-va-rachnii chai-nik*

teaspoon чайная ложка *chai-naya losch-ka*

teeth зубы *zu-bi*

telegram телеграмма *tili-gra-ma*

telephone[1] *n* телефон *tili-fon*

telephone[2] *vb* звонить *zva-nit'*

telephone box телефонная будка *tili-fon-naya but-ka*

telephone call телефонный звонок *tili-fon-nii zva-nok*

telephone directory телефонная книга *tili-fon-naya kni-ga*

television телевидение *tili-vi-dyenye*

television set телевизор *tili-vi-zar*

telex телекс *tye-liks*

tell говорить *gava-rit'*

temperature температура *timpira-tu-ra* ; **I have a temperature** у меня температура *umi-nya timpira-tu-ra*

temporary временный *vrye-minii*

tennis теннис *te-nis*

tennis court теннисный корт *te-nisnii kort*

tennis racket теннисная ракетка *te-nisnaya ra-kyet-ka*

tent палатка *pa-lat-ka*

tent peg колышки для палатки *ko-lischki dlya pa-lat-ki*

terminus *(for buses)* конечная

остановка ka-**nyech**-naya asta-**nof**-ka; (station) вокзал vak-**zal**

terrace терраса ti-**ra**-sa

than: better than this лучше чем это **lut**-sche chyem e-ta

thank you спасибо spa-**si**-ba; **thank you very much** большое спасибо bal'-**scho**-ye spa-**si**-ba

that тот tot; **that one** вон тот von tot

thaw: it's thawing тает ta-yet

theatre театр ti-**atr**

then тогда ta-**gda**; **they will be away then** в это время их не будет ve-ta **vrye**-mya ikh ni **bu**-dit

there там tam

thermometer градусник **gra**-dusnik

these эти e-ti

they они a-**ni**

thief вор vor

thing вещь vyesh; **my things** мои вещи mai vye-**shchi**

think думать **du**-mat'

third третий **trye**-tii

thirsty: I'm thirsty я хочу пить ya kha-**chu** pit'

this m/f/nt этот/эта/это e-tat/e-ta/e-to

those эти e-ti

thread нитка **nit**-ka

throat горло **gor**-la

throat lozenges ментоловые пастилки min-**to**-lavii pas-**til**-ki

through насквозь na-**skvos**'; (ticket) прямой pri-**moi**

thunderstorm гроза gra-**za**

ticket билет bi-**lyet**

ticket collector кондуктор kan-**duk**-tar

ticket office касса **ka**-sa

tie галстук **gals**-tuk

tights колготки kal-**got**-ki

till[1] n касса **ka**-sa

till[2] conj (until) пока pa-**ka**

time время **vrye**-mya; **this time** на этот раз na e-tat ras

timetable расписание raspi-**sa**-niye

tin банка **ban**-ka

tinfoil жесть zhest'

tin-opener консервный нож kan-**syerv**-nii nosch

tip (to waiter, etc) чаевые chaye-**vi**-ye

tired усталый us-**ta**-lii

tissue бумажные салфетки bu-**mazh**-nii sal-**fyet**-ki

to: to London в Лондон vlon-**dan**; **to Spain** в Испанию vis-pa-**niyu**

toast тост tost

tobacco табак ta-**bak**

tobacconist's табачные изделия ta-**bach**-nii iz-**dye**-liya

today сегодня si-**vod**-nya

together вместе **vmyes**-ti

toilet туалет tua-**lyet**

toilet paper туалетная бумага tua-**lyet**-naya bu-**ma**-ga

tomato помидор pami-**dor**

tomato juice томатный сок ta-**mat**-nii sok

tomorrow завтра **zaf**-tra

tongue язык ya-**zik**

tonic water тоник **to**-nik

tonight сегодня вечером si-**vod**-nya **vye**-chiram

too (also) тоже *to-zhe*; **it's too big** слишком велик *slisch-kam vi-lik*

tooth зуб *zup*

toothache: I have toothache у меня болят зубы *umi-nya ba-lyat zu-bi*

toothbrush зубная щетка *zub-na-ya shchot-ka*

toothpaste зубная паста *zub-na-ya pas-ta*

top¹ adj : **the top floor** верхний этаж *vyerkh-nii e-tasch*

top² n верх *vyerkh*; **on top of…** наверху *navir-khu*

torch фонарик *fa-na-rik*

torn порваный *po-rvanii*

total всего *fsye-vo*

tough (meat) жесткий *zhost-kii*

tour тур *tur*

tourist турист *tu-rist*

tourist office турбюро *turbyu-ro*

tourist ticket туристский билет *tu-ris-kii bi-lyet*

tow буксировать *buk-si-ravat'*

towel полотенце *pala-tyen-tse*

town город *go-rat*

town centre центр города *tsentr go-rada*

town plan план города *plan go-rada*

towrope (буксирный) трос *(buk-sir-nii) tros*

toy игрушка *ig-rusch-ka*

traditional традиционный *traditsi-on-nii*

traffic движение *dvi-zhe-niye*

train поезд *po-ist*

tram трамвай *tram-vai*

translate переводить *piriva-dit'*

translation перевод *piri-vot*

travel путешествовать *puti-schest-vavat'*

traveller's cheques дорожные чеки *da-rozh-nii chye-ki*

tray поднос *pad-nos*

tree дерево *dye-riva*

trim подравнивать *pad-rav-nivat'*

trip поездка *pa-yest-ka*

trouble n неприятность *nipri-yat-nast'*

trousers брюки *bryu-ki*

true правда *prav-da*

trunk (luggage) сундук *sun-duk*

trunks плавки *plaf-ki*

try пробовать *pro-bavat'*

try on примерять *primi-ryat'*

tuna тунец *tu-nyets*

tunnel тоннель *ta-nel'*

turkey индейка *in-dyei-ka*

turn (handle, wheel) поворачивать *pava-ra-chivat'*

turnip турнепс *tur-neps*

turn off (radio, etc) выключать *viklyu-chat'*; (tap) завернуть *zavir-nut'*

turn on (light, etc) включать *fklyu-chat'*; (tap) отвернуть *atvir-nut'*

tweezers щипчики *shchip-chiki*

twice дважды *dvazh-di*

twin-bedded room номер на двоих *no-mir na dva-ikh*

typical типичный *ti-pich-nii*

tyre шина *schi-na*

tyre pressure давление в шинах *dav-lye-niye fschi-nakh*

umbrella зонтик *zon-tik*

uncomfortable неудобный *nyeu-dob-nii*

unconscious бессознательный *byessaz-na-tyel'nii*

under под *pot*

underground (metro) метро *mit-ro*

underpass подземный переход *pad-zyem-nii piri-khot*

understand понимать *pani-mat'* ; **I don't understand** я не понимаю *ya ni pani-ma-yu*

underwear нижнее белье *nizh-nyeye bil'-yo*

union союз *sa-yus*

United States Соединенные Штаты *saidi-nyo-nii schta-ti*

university университет *univirsi-tyet*

unpack (case) распаковывать *raspa-ko-vivat'*

up: up there там наверху *tam navir-khu*

upstairs наверх *na-vyerkh*

urgent срочный *sroch-nii*

USA США *se-sche-a*

use использовать *is-pol'-zavat'*

useful полезный *pa-lyez-nii*

usual обычный *a-bich-nii*

usually обычно *a-bich-na*

vacuum cleaner пылесос *pilye-sos*

valid действительный *dist-vi-tyel'nii*

valley долина *da-li-na*

valuable ценный *tsen-nii*

valuables ценности *tsen-nasti*

van фургон *fur-gon*

vase ваза *va-za*

veal телятина *ti-lya-tina*

vegetables овощи *o-vashchi*

vegetarian n вегетарианец *vigitari-a-nits*

very очень *o-chin'*

vest майка *mai-ka*

via через *che-ris*

village деревня *di-ryev-nya*

vinegar уксус *uk-sus*

vineyard виноградник *vina-grad-nik*

visa виза *vi-za*

visit визит *vi-zit*

vitamin витамин *vita-min*

vodka водка *vot-ka*

voltage напряжение *napri-zhe-niye*

waist талия *ta-liya*

wait (for) ждать *zhdat'*

waiter официант *afitsi-ant*

waiting room зал ожидания *zal azhi-da-niya*

waitress официантка *afitsi-ant-ka*

wake up просыпаться *prasi-pat-sa*

Wales Уэльс *u-el's*

walk vb гулять *gu-lyat'* ; **to go for a walk** идти гулять *it-ti gu-lyat'*

wallet бумажник *bu-mazh-nik*

walnut грецкий орех *gryets-kii a-ryekh*

want хотеть *kha-tyet'*

warm теплый *tyop-lii*

warning triangle предупреждающий треугольник *priduprizh-da-yushii triu-gol'-nik*

wash стирать *sti-rat'*; **to wash oneself** мыться *mit-sa*; **to wash up** мыть посуду *mit' pa-su-du*

washbasin раковина *ra-kavina*

washing powder стиральный порошок *sti-ral'-nii para-schok*

washing-up liquid средство для мытья посуды *sryet-stva dlya mi-tya pa-su-di*

wasp оса *a-sa*

waste bin урна *ur-na*

watch[1] *n* часы *chi-si*

watch[2] *vb* (look at) смотреть *smat-ryet'*; (look after) смотреть за *smat-ryet' za*; **watch out!** осторожно! *asta-rozh-na*

water вода *va-da*

waterfall водопад *vada-pat*

watermelon арбуз *ar-bus*

waterproof водонепроницаемый *vodaniprani-tsa-yemii*

water-skiing водные лыжи *vod-nii li-zhi*

wave (on sea) волна *val-na*

wax *n* воск *vosk*

way (manner) манера *ma-nye-ra*; (route) путь *put'*; **this way** сюда *syu-da*

we мы *mi*

weak слабый *sla-bii*

wear носить *na-sit'*

weather погода *pa-go-da*

wedding свадьба *svad'-ba*

week неделя *ni-dye-lya*

weekday рабочий день *ra-bo-chii dyen'*

weekend конец недели *ka-nyets ni-dye-li*

weekly (rate, etc) еженедельный *yezhini-dyel'-nii*

weight вес *vyes*

welcome! добро пожаловать! *da-bro pa-zha-lavat'*

well: he's not well он плохо себя чувствует *on plo-kha si-bya chust-vuyet*; **well-done** (steak) зажаренный *za-zha-rinii*

Welsh *m/f/adj* валлиец/валлийка/ валлийский *va-li-its/va-lii-ka/va-lii-skii*

west запад *za-pat*

wet мокрый *mok-rii*

what что *schto*; **what is it?** что это? *schto e-ta*

wheel колесо *kali-so*

wheelchair инвалидная коляска *inva-lid-naya ka-lyas-ka*

when когда *kag-da*

where где *gdye*

which: which is it? какой это? *ka-koi e-ta*

while: can you do it while I wait? можно это сделать пока я жду? *mozh-na e-ta zdye-lat' pa-ka ya zhdy*

whisky виски *vis-ki*

white белый *bye-lii*

who: who is it? кто это? *kto e-ta*

whole целый *tsye-lii*

whose: whose is it? чье это? *chyo e-ta*

why почему *pachi-mu*

wide широкий *schi-ro-kii*

wife жена *zhi-na*

window окно *ak-no*; (shop) витрина *vi-tri-na*

windscreen ветровое стекло *vyetra-vo-ye stik-lo*

windsurfing виндсерфинг *vint-ser-fink*

windy: it's windy ветрено *vye-trino*

wine вино *vi-no*

wine list список вин *spi-sak vin*

winter зима *zi-ma*

with с *s*

without без *byes*

woman женщина *zhen-shchina*

wood (material) дерево *dye-riva*; (forest) лес *lyes*

wool шерсть *scherst'*

word слово *slo-va*

work[1] *n* работа *ra-bo-ta*

work[2] *vb* (person, machine) работать *ra-bo-tat'*

worried беспокойный *bispa-koi-nii*

worse хуже *khu-zhi*

worth: it's worth the price это стоит этих денег *e-ta sto-it e-tikh dye-nik*

wrap (up) заворачивать *zava-ra-chivat'*

wrapping paper оберточная бумага *a-byor-tachnaya bu-ma-ga*

write писать *pi-sat'*

writing paper бумага для письма *bu-ma-ga dlya pis'-ma*

wrong неверный *ni-vyer-nii*; sorry, **wrong number** извините, не тот номер *izvi-ni-tye ni tot no-myer*

x-ray рентген *rin-gyen*

yacht яхта *yakh-ta*

year год *got*

yellow желтый *zhol-tii*

yes да *da*; yes, please да, пожалуйста *da pa-zha-lusta*

yesterday вчера *fchi-ra*

yet: not yet нет еще *nyet ye-shcho*

yoghurt фруктовый кефир *fruk-to-vii ki-fir*

you (with friends) ты *ti*; (formal, plural) вы *vi*

young молодой *mala-doi*

youth hostel молодежная гостиница *mala-dyozh-naya gas-ti-nitsa*

zero ноль *nol'*

zip молния *mol-niya*

zoo зоопарк *zaa-park*

абонемент season ticket (*cinema, swimming pool, etc*)

абрикос apricot

абсурд absurdity

аванс deposit (*money*)

аварийный/ая *adj* emergency; **аварийная машина** breakdown van; **аварийный ремонт** emergency repair; **аварийный выход** emergency exit

авария accident; crash

август August

авиа- *adj* air(-)

авиабилет airplane ticket

авиалиния airline

авиапочта air mail

авиация aviation

автобаза motor depot

автобиография autobiography

автобус bus; coach; **остановка автобуса** bus stop

автовокзал bus station

автолюбитель car owner

автомат automatic machine; **билетный автомат** ticket machine

автомобиль car

автопортрет self-portrait

автор author

авторучка fountain pen

автострада motorway

автотурист/ка *m/f* tourist (*in car*)

агенство agency; **телеграфное агенство** news agency

ад hell

администрация management

адмирал admiral

Адмиралтейство Admiralty

адрес address

адресный/ая *adj* address; **адресный стол** address bureau; **адресная книга** directory

Азия Asia

А	а	А
Б	б	Б
В	в	В
Г	г	Г
Д	д	Д
Е	е	Е
Ё	ё	Ё
Ж	ж	Ж
З	з	З
И	и	И
Й	й	Й
К	к	К
Л	л	Л
М	м	М
Н	н	Н
О	о	О
П	п	П
Р	р	Р
С	с	С
Т	т	Т
У	у	У
Ф	ф	Ф
Х	х	Х
Ц	ц	Ц
Ч	ч	Ч
Ш	ш	Ш
Щ	щ	Щ
Ъ	ъ	Ъ
Ы	ы	Ы
Ь	ь	Ь
Э	э	Э
Ю	ю	Ю
Я	я	Я

академия academy

аквамарин aquamarine (stone)

аквариум aquarium

акт act (theatre)

актер/актриса actor/actress

активно actively

алкоголь alcohol; spirits

алкогольный/ая adj alcoholic; **алкогольные напитки** wines and spirits

аллея alley

Алтай Altai

алфавит alphabet

альбом album; **альбом для фотографий** photo album

альпинизм mountaineering

Америка America

американский/ая adj American

аметист amethyst (stone)

анализ analysis; sample; **анализ крови** blood test

английский/ая adj English

Англия England

ансамбль ensemble; **ансамбль песни и пляски** folk singing and dancing group

антракт intermission (circus)

аппарат apparatus; **фотоаппарат** camera

апрель April

аптека chemist's

армия army

Армения Armenia

аспирин aspirin

ассорти assortment

ателье dressmaker; tailor; **ателье мод** fashion house; **ателье проката** rental/hire services

аттестат certificate

аукцион auction

аэропорт airport

А	а	А
Б	б	Б
В	в	В
Г	г	Г
Д	д	Д
Е	е	Е
Ё	ё	Ё
Ж	ж	Ж
З	з	З
И	и	И
Й	й	Й
К	к	К
Л	л	Л
М	м	М
Н	н	Н
О	о	О
П	п	П
Р	р	Р
С	с	С
Т	т	Т
У	у	У
Ф	ф	Ф
Х	х	Х
Ц	ц	Ц
Ч	ч	Ч
Ш	ш	Ш
Щ	щ	Щ
Ъ	ъ	Ъ
Ы	ы	Ы
Ь	ь	Ь
Э	э	Э
Ю	ю	Ю
Я	я	Я

Баба-Яга Baba-Yaga *(witch in Russian folk tales)*

бабушка grandma

багаж luggage; **выдача багажа** baggage reclaim; **ручной багаж** hand luggage

базар market

бакалея grocery

баклажан aubergine

бал ball; dancing party

балет ballet

Балтийское Море Baltic Sea

банк bank; **Внешэкономбанк** Foreign Trade Bank; **акционерный банк** joint-stock bank

банкет banquet; **банкетный зал** function room *(hotels, etc)*

баня public baths

бар bar

баранина lamb *(meat)*

басня fable

бассейн swimming pool

батон white bread stick

башня tower

бег running

безработица unemployment

белка squirrel

Белоруссия Byelorussia

белый/ая white; **белое вино** white wine

белье linen; **нижнее белье** underwear; **постельное белье** bedclothes

бензин petrol

бензоколонка petrol station

библиотека library

Библия Biblia

бижутерия jewellery

билет ticket; **пригласительный билет** invitation card

билетная касса booking office

бинт bandage

бирюза turquoise *(stone)*

А	а	А
Б	б	Б
В	в	В
Г	г	Г
Д	д	Д
Е	е	Е
Ё	ё	Ё
Ж	ж	Ж
З	з	З
И	и	И
Й	й	Й
К	к	К
Л	л	Л
М	м	М
Н	н	Н
О	о	О
П	п	П
Р	р	Р
С	с	С
Т	т	Т
У	у	У
Ф	ф	Ф
Х	х	Х
Ц	ц	Ц
Ч	ч	Ч
Ш	ш	Ш
Щ	щ	Щ
Ъ	ъ	Ъ
Ы	ы	Ы
Ь	ь	Ь
Э	э	Э
Ю	ю	Ю
Я	я	Я

бисквит sponge-cake
бифштекс (beef)steak
благодарность gratitude
блин pancake; **блинная** pancake house
блокада siege
блюдо dish; **обед из трех блюд** three-course lunch
Бог God
Богородица Our Lady
бокал goblet *(champagne glass)*
больница hospital
брак marriage
бракованный/ая defective
брат brother
бриллиант diamond
бритва razor
брюки trousers
будильник alarm clock
буква letter *(a, b, c, etc)*; **букварь** primer
булка wheat loaf (small)
булочная baker's
бульон clear soup
бумага paper
буфет buffet
быстро fast; quickly
бюро office; **справочное бюро** information office; **бюро находок** lost property office
бюстгалтер bra

вагон carriage *(train)*; **спальный вагон** sleeper; **вагон-ресторан** dining-car
валюта currency; **иностранная валюта** hard currency
ванна bath
вареник curd dumpling
варенье jam
вата cotton wool
вежливый/ая polite

А	а	А
Б	б	Б
В	в	В
Г	г	Г
Д	д	Д
Е	е	Е
Ё	ё	Ё
Ж	ж	Ж
З	з	З
И	и	И
Й	й	Й
К	к	К
Л	л	Л
М	м	М
Н	н	Н
О	о	О
П	п	П
Р	р	Р
С	с	С
Т	т	Т
У	у	У
Ф	ф	Ф
Х	х	Х
Ц	ц	Ц
Ч	ч	Ч
Ш	ш	Ш
Щ	щ	Щ
Ъ	ъ	Ъ
Ы	ы	Ы
Ь	ь	Ь
Э	э	Э
Ю	ю	Ю
Я	я	Я

век century
великан giant
великий/ая great; **Петр Великий** Peter the Great
велосипед bicycle
вертолет helicopter
верх top
верховая езда horse riding
вес weight; **весы** scales
виза visa
викторина quiz show
вилка fork
винегрет vegetable salad
вино wine; **белое вино** white wine; **красное вино** red wine; **сухое вино** dry wine; **сладкое вино** sweet wine
виноград grapes
вишня cherry
вкусный/ая tasty
власть power; authority
внимание attention
вода water; **минеральная вода** mineral water
водка vodka
военный/ая military
вождь leader
воздух air
Возрождение Renaissance
война war
вокзал railway station; terminus; **морской вокзал** seaport
вокруг around
волна wave
волнорез breakwater
волокно fibre
волосы hair
волшебный/ая magical
вопрос question
вор thief; pickpocket

А	а	А
Б	б	Б
В	в	В
Г	г	Г
Д	д	Д
Е	е	Е
Ё	ё	Ё
Ж	ж	Ж
З	з	З
И	и	И
Й	й	Й
К	к	К
Л	л	Л
М	м	М
Н	н	Н
О	о	О
П	п	П
Р	р	Р
С	с	С
Т	т	Т
У	у	У
Ф	ф	Ф
Х	х	Х
Ц	ц	Ц
Ч	ч	Ч
Ш	ш	Ш
Щ	щ	Щ
Ъ	ъ	Ъ
Ы	ы	Ы
Ь	ь	Ь
Э	э	Э
Ю	ю	Ю
Я	я	Я

ворота gates

воспаление inflammation; **воспаление легких** pneumonia

воспрещать to prohibit; **посторонним вход воспрещен!** no unauthorized entry!; **курить воспрещается!** no smoking!

восстание revolt

восток east; **Дальний Восток** Far East; **Ближний Восток** Middle East

вперед forward; ahead

впуск admittance

врач doctor *(medical)*

вредить to harm; to damage

время time; **свободное время** leisure time

всегда always

все everybody; everything; all

вселенная universe

всемерно in any possible way

всенародный/ая nationwide

всенощная evening service *(church)*

всеобщий/ая general; universal

вспышка flash *(camera)*

встреча meeting

вступать to enter; to join

вход entrance; **вход свободный** admission free; **вход по билетам** admission by ticket only

входить to enter

вчера yesterday

въезд entrance *(for cars)*

выборы election

выдача distribution; **выдача багажа** luggage reclaim

выезд exit *(for cars)*

выигрыш prize

выключать to switch off

вылет departures *(by plane)*

выпуск issue

выражать to express *(an idea)*

А	а	А
Б	б	Б
В	в	В
Г	г	Г
Д	д	Д
Е	е	Е
Ё	ё	Ё
Ж	ж	Ж
З	з	З
И	и	И
Й	й	Й
К	к	К
Л	л	Л
М	м	М
Н	н	Н
О	о	О
П	п	П
Р	р	Р
С	с	С
Т	т	Т
У	у	У
Ф	ф	Ф
Х	х	Х
Ц	ц	Ц
Ч	ч	Ч
Ш	ш	Ш
Щ	щ	Щ
Ъ	ъ	Ъ
Ы	ы	Ы
Ь	ь	Ь
Э	э	Э
Ю	ю	Ю
Я	я	Я

ВЫС – ГЛА

высокий/ая high; tall
выставка exhibition; **выставочный зал** exhibition hall
высший/ая higher; superior
вытрезвитель sobering-up station
выход exit
выходной день day off
вязание knitting; **вязание крючком** crochet

гавань harbour
газ gas
газета newspaper
газетный киоск newsstand
газированная вода sparkling water
газон lawn; **по газонам не ходить!** keep off the grass!
ГАИ traffic police (post)
галерея gallery; **картинная галерея** art gallery
галстук tie; cravat
гараж garage
гарантировать to guarantee
гарантия guarantee
гардероб cloakroom
гарнитур suite; set
гастроли tour
гастроном groceries
где where
генерал general (in army)
Германия Germany
герой hero
гибкий/ая flexible
гигант giant
гигиенический/ая hygienic; **гигиенические прокладки** sanitary towels
гимн hymn
гимназия gymnasia
гинеколог gynaecologist
главный/ая main; chief

А	а	А
Б	б	Б
В	в	В
Г	г	Г
Д	д	Д
Е	е	Е
Ё	ё	Ё
Ж	ж	Ж
З	з	З
И	и	И
Й	й	Й
К	к	К
Л	л	Л
М	м	М
Н	н	Н
О	о	О
П	п	П
Р	р	Р
С	с	С
Т	т	Т
У	у	У
Ф	ф	Ф
Х	х	Х
Ц	ц	Ц
Ч	ч	Ч
Ш	ш	Ш
Щ	щ	Щ
Ъ	ъ	Ъ
Ы	ы	Ы
Ь	ь	Ь
Э	э	Э
Ю	ю	Ю
Я	я	Я

глаз eye
гласность openness
глубокий/ая deep
говорить to say
говядина beef
год year
годовой/ая annual; yearly
голова head
голодный/ая hungry
гололед/ица black ice *(on road)*
голос voice
голосовать to vote
голубой/ая light blue
голый/ая naked
гонки car race
гора mountain
гордый/ая proud
горе grief
горло throat
горничная chambermaid
город city; town
горчица mustard
горький/ая bitter
горячий/ая hot
Госбанк State Bank
господин gentleman; Mr
госпожа lady; Mrs
Госстрах National Insurance Office
гостиная lounge
гостиница hotel
Гостиный Двор Gostiny Dvor *(Merchant's House department store)*
гость guest
государство state
готовый/ая ready-made
гравер engraver

А	а	А
Б	б	Б
В	в	В
Г	г	Г
Д	д	Д
Е	е	Е
Ё	ё	Ё
Ж	ж	Ж
З	з	З
И	и	И
Й	й	Й
К	к	К
Л	л	Л
М	м	М
Н	н	Н
О	о	О
П	п	П
Р	р	Р
С	с	С
Т	т	Т
У	у	У
Ф	ф	Ф
Х	х	Х
Ц	ц	Ц
Ч	ч	Ч
Ш	ш	Ш
Щ	щ	Щ
Ъ	ъ	Ъ
Ы	ы	Ы
Ь	ь	Ь
Э	э	Э
Ю	ю	Ю
Я	я	Я

гравюра engraving
градус degree
гражданин citizen (male)
гражданка citizen (female)
гражданство citizenship
грамзапись record; LP
грамм gram
грамматика grammar
грампластинка record; LP
граница border; frontier
график schedule
графика drawing
грейпфрут grapefruit
грецкий орех walnut
греча buckwheat
гриб mushroom
грильяж sugar-coated nuts/almonds
грипп flu; influenza
громкий/ая loud
гроссмейстер grand chess master
грубый/ая rough; rude
грудь breast; chest
груз load; goods
группа group
груша pear
грязный/ая dirty
губа lip; **губная помада** lipstick
гулянье outdoor festival
гуманитарные науки the Arts; the Humanities
гусь goose

да yes; **да здравствует...!** long live...!
давайте let us ...
давление pressure
давно long ago
Дальний Восток Far East

А	а	А
Б	б	Б
В	в	В
Г	г	Г
Д	д	Д
Е	е	Е
Ё	ё	Ё
Ж	ж	Ж
З	з	З
И	и	И
Й	й	Й
К	к	К
Л	л	Л
М	м	М
Н	н	Н
О	о	О
П	п	П
Р	р	Р
С	с	С
Т	т	Т
У	у	У
Ф	ф	Ф
Х	х	Х
Ц	ц	Ц
Ч	ч	Ч
Ш	ш	Ш
Щ	щ	Щ
Ъ	ъ	Ъ
Ы	ы	Ы
Ь	ь	Ь
Э	э	Э
Ю	ю	Ю
Я	я	Я

дама lady

дамский/ая lady's; female

дарить to give a present

дарование talent

дата date

дача country house

дверь door

двигатель engine

движение movement; traffic

двойной/ая double

двойня twins

двор court; coutryard

дворец palace; **Дворец Культуры** Palace of Culture

двуспальный/ая double; **двуспальная кровать** double bed

двухкомнатный/ая two-roomed

двухместный/ая two-seater; double

девиз motto

девочка little girl

девушка young girl; Miss

дедушка grandfather

дежурный/ая on duty *(person)*

действие action; act

декабрь December

декларация declaration

декоративно-прикладное искусство arts and crafts

декрет decree; edict

делать to do

делегат delegate

делегация delegation

дело business

демисезонный/ая *adj* spring/autumn; **демисезонное пальто** light overcoat

демократический/ая democratic

демонстрационный зал showroom

демонстрация demonstration

А	а	А
Б	б	Б
В	в	В
Г	г	Г
Д	д	Д
Е	е	Е
Ё	ё	Ё
Ж	ж	Ж
З	з	З
И	и	И
Й	й	Й
К	к	К
Л	л	Л
М	м	М
Н	н	Н
О	о	О
П	п	П
Р	р	Р
С	с	С
Т	т	Т
У	у	У
Ф	ф	Ф
Х	х	Х
Ц	ц	Ц
Ч	ч	Ч
Ш	ш	Ш
Щ	щ	Щ
Ъ	ъ	Ъ
Ы	ы	Ы
Ь	ь	Ь
Э	э	Э
Ю	ю	Ю
Я	я	Я

денежно-вещевая лотерея cash and prize lottery
день day; **рабочий день** working day
деньги money
депо depot
депозит deposit
депутат deputy
деревня village
дерево tree
деревянный/ая wooden
держать to keep; to hold
десерт dessert
десяток ten
детдом orphanage
детектив detective
дети chidren
детский/ая children's; **детский сад** nursery school
дефицит shortage
дешевый/ая cheap
деятельность activities
джаз jazz
джем jam; confiture
джемпер jumper
джинсы jeans
диабетический/ая *adj* diabetic
диагноз diagnosis
диаметр diameter
диафильм film strip; slides
диван sofa; settee; **диван-кровать** folding sofa
диета diet
диетический/ая *adj* diet; **диетическое питание** diet food
дизель diesel engine
дикий/ая wild
диктатура dictatorship
динамо dynamo
директор director; **директор школы** headmaster/
  mistress

А	а	А
Б	б	Б
В	в	В
Г	г	Г
Д	д	Д
Е	е	Е
Ё	ё	Ё
Ж	ж	Ж
З	з	З
И	и	И
Й	й	Й
К	к	К
Л	л	Л
М	м	М
Н	н	Н
О	о	О
П	п	П
Р	р	Р
С	с	С
Т	т	Т
У	у	У
Ф	ф	Ф
Х	х	Х
Ц	ц	Ц
Ч	ч	Ч
Ш	ш	Ш
Щ	щ	Щ
Ъ	ъ	Ъ
Ы	ы	Ы
Ь	ь	Ь
Э	э	Э
Ю	ю	Ю
Я	я	Я

дирижер conductor *(music)*
диск disk
дискотека disco
дискуссия discussion
диспансер outpatient clinic
диспут public debate
дистанция distance; **соблюдай дистанцию!** keep your distance!
длина length
для for
дневник diary
дно bottom *(pool, etc)*
добиваться to achieve
добро good; things
добрый/ая good; kind; **добро пожаловать!** welcome!; **добрый день!** good day!; **всего доброго!** all the best!
доверие trust
договор agreement
договорный/ая agreed; contractual; **договорные цены** contractual prices
дождь rain
доктор doctor; Doctor of…
документ document; **фото на документы** passport-size photo
долг debt
долгий/ая long
долина valley
доллар dollar
дом house
дома at home
домашний/яя domestic; household
домкрат jack *(for car)*
дорога road; **железная дорога** railway
дорогой/ая expensive; dear
доска board; **шахматная доска** chessboard
досмотр: таможенный досмотр customs examination
досрочно ahead of time

А	а	А
Б	б	Б
В	в	В
Г	г	Г
Д	д	Д
Е	е	Е
Ё	ё	Ё
Ж	ж	Ж
З	з	З
И	и	И
Й	й	Й
К	к	К
Л	л	Л
М	м	М
Н	н	Н
О	о	О
П	п	П
Р	р	Р
С	с	С
Т	т	Т
У	у	У
Ф	ф	Ф
Х	х	Х
Ц	ц	Ц
Ч	ч	Ч
Ш	ш	Ш
Щ	щ	Щ
Ъ	ъ	Ъ
Ы	ы	Ы
Ь	ь	Ь
Э	э	Э
Ю	ю	Ю
Я	я	Я

досуг leisure

доход income

дочь daughter

дошкольник child *(pre-school)*

драгоценности jewellery

драма drama

драматический театр drama theatre

дрессированный/ая trained; **дрессированные звери** circus animals

друг friend *(male)*

дуб oak

дублированный/ая dubbed

дурак/дура *m/f* fool

духовой/ая wind *(musical)*; **духовой оркестр** brass brand

душ shower

дуэль dual

дым smoke

дыня melon

дядя uncle

Евангелие Gospel

Европа Europe

еда food

еженедельник weekly magazine

езда ride; drive; **езда на лошадях** horse riding

елка fir tree

если if

естественный/ая natural

жакет jacket

жалоба complaint; **книга жалоб и предложений** complaints and suggestions book

жара heat

жареный/ая fried

жаркий/ая hot

А	а	А
Б	б	Б
В	в	В
Г	г	Г
Д	д	Д
Е	е	Е
Ё	ё	Ё
Ж	ж	Ж
З	з	З
И	и	И
Й	й	Й
К	к	К
Л	л	Л
М	м	М
Н	н	Н
О	о	О
П	п	П
Р	р	Р
С	с	С
Т	т	Т
У	у	У
Ф	ф	Ф
Х	х	Х
Ц	ц	Ц
Ч	ч	Ч
Ш	ш	Ш
Щ	щ	Щ
Ъ	ъ	Ъ
Ы	ы	Ы
Ь	ь	Ь
Э	э	Э
Ю	ю	Ю
Я	я	Я

жар-птица the fire-bird *(folklore)*

жвачка chewing gum

ждать to wait

желание wish

желе jelly

железный/ая *adj* iron; **железная дорога** railway

желтый/ая yellow

жемчуг pearl

жена wife

жених fiancé; bridegroom

женский/ая women's; female

женщина woman; **товары для женщин** goods for women

жесткий/ая hard; tough; **жесткий вагон** second-class carriage

живой/ая alive; living; **живая рыба** fresh fish

живопись painting; **акварельная живопись** watercolour painting

живот stomach

животное animal

жидкий/ая *adj* liquid

жизнь life

жилет waistcoat

жилище dwelling

жилой/ая residential

жир fat; grease

житель resident *(male)*

жительница resident *(female)*

жить to leave

жонглер juggler

журавль crane *(bird)*

журнальный/ая *adj* magazine; **журнальный столик** coffee table

ЖЭК housing office *(for maintenance)*

забава amusement; fun

забастовка strike

А	а	А
Б	б	Б
В	в	В
Г	г	Г
Д	д	Д
Е	е	Е
Ё	ё	Ё
Ж	ж	Ж
З	з	З
И	и	И
Й	й	Й
К	к	К
Л	л	Л
М	м	М
Н	н	Н
О	о	О
П	п	П
Р	р	Р
С	с	С
Т	т	Т
У	у	У
Ф	ф	Ф
Х	х	Х
Ц	ц	Ц
Ч	ч	Ч
Ш	ш	Ш
Щ	щ	Щ
Ъ	ъ	Ъ
Ы	ы	Ы
Ь	ь	Ь
Э	э	Э
Ю	ю	Ю
Я	я	Я

заболевание disease
заботиться to look after
заварка strong tea
заведующий/ая manager/manageress
заверять to witness; to certify
завещание will (document)
завивка blow-dry; **шестимесячная завивка** perm
завод works; plant
заводной/ая mechanical; **заводная игрушка** clockwork toy
завоз delivery of goods
завтра tomorrow
завтрак breakfast
загадка riddle; enigma
загар suntan; **крем для загара** suntan lotion; **крем от загара** sun block
заговор plot (political)
заголовок headline
загорать to sunbathe
загородный/ая out of town
заготовка laying in; stockpiling
заграница foreign countries
заграничный/ая foreign; **заграничный паспорт** external passport
ЗАГС registry office
зад rear
задание task
задача problem
задержка delay
зажигалка lighter
зажигание ignition
заказной/ая registered (mail)
закон law
закрыто closed
зал hall; **зрительный зал** auditorium; **концертный зал** concert hall
залив bay; **Финский залив** Gulf of Finland

А	а	А
Б	б	Б
В	в	В
Г	г	Г
Д	д	Д
Е	е	Е
Ё	ё	Ё
Ж	ж	Ж
З	з	З
И	и	И
Й	й	Й
К	к	К
Л	л	Л
М	м	М
Н	н	Н
О	о	О
П	п	П
Р	р	Р
С	с	С
Т	т	Т
У	у	У
Ф	ф	Ф
Х	х	Х
Ц	ц	Ц
Ч	ч	Ч
Ш	ш	Ш
Щ	щ	Щ
Ъ	ъ	Ъ
Ы	ы	Ы
Ь	ь	Ь
Э	э	Э
Ю	ю	Ю
Я	я	Я

заливное fish/meat in aspic
замена replacement
замок castle; lock
замша suede
занавеска curtain
запад west
запас stock
запасной выход emergency exit
записная книжка note book
заповедник national park
запрещать to forbid; **курить запрещается!** no smoking!
запчасти spare parts
зарплата wages; salary
заря dawn
зарядка recharge *(battery, lighter)*; morning exercise
застолье feast
защита defence
заявление statement; written request
заяц hair; passenger without ticket
звезда star
зверь wild animal
звонок bell
здесь here
здорово! hi!
здоровый/ая healthy
здравоохранение public health service
здравствуйте! how do you do?; hello!;
    да здравствует...! long live ...!
зеленый/ая green
земля earth
зеркало mirror
зерно grain
зима winter
зло evil
знакомый/ая *m/f* acquaintance; friend
знание knowledge

А	а	А
Б	б	Б
В	в	В
Г	г	Г
Д	д	Д
Е	е	Е
Ё	ё	Ё
Ж	ж	Ж
З	з	З
И	и	И
Й	й	Й
К	к	К
Л	л	Л
М	м	М
Н	н	Н
О	о	О
П	п	П
Р	р	Р
С	с	С
Т	т	Т
У	у	У
Ф	ф	Ф
Х	х	Х
Ц	ц	Ц
Ч	ч	Ч
Ш	ш	Ш
Щ	щ	Щ
Ъ	ъ	Ъ
Ы	ы	Ы
Ь	ь	Ь
Э	э	Э
Ю	ю	Ю
Я	я	Я

знать to know

значение meaning

значок badge; pin

Зодиак Zodiac; **знаки зодиака** signs of the zodiac

зодчий architect

золото gold

зонтик umbrella

зоомагазин pet shop

зоопарк zoo

зрелище show

зрение eyesight

зритель spectator

зрительный зал auditorium

зуб(ы) tooth (teeth)

зубной врач dentist

и and

игла needle

игра game; **Олимпийские Игры** Olympic Games

играть to play

идея idea

идти to go

изба peasant log hut

известный/ая famous

Известия news

издание publication

издательство publishing house

изделие produce; article; **изделия из льна** linen goods

изобразительное искусство fine arts

изумруд emerald *(stone)*

изучать to study

изюм raisins

икона icon

икра caviar

или or

иллюзионист magician

А	а	А
Б	б	Б
В	в	В
Г	г	Г
Д	д	Д
Е	е	Е
Ё	ё	Ё
Ж	ж	Ж
З	з	З
И	и	И
Й	й	Й
К	к	К
Л	л	Л
М	м	М
Н	н	Н
О	о	О
П	п	П
Р	р	Р
С	с	С
Т	т	Т
У	у	У
Ф	ф	Ф
Х	х	Х
Ц	ц	Ц
Ч	ч	Ч
Ш	ш	Ш
Щ	щ	Щ
Ъ	ъ	Ъ
Ы	ы	Ы
Ь	ь	Ь
Э	э	Э
Ю	ю	Ю
Я	я	Я

ИМЕ – ЙОД

имение manor
иметь to have
имя name
инвалид disabled person
индейка turkey
индекс postcode
инженер engineer
инкрустация inlaid work
институт higher education establishment
инструменты tools
интересный/ая interesting
интернациональный/ая international
интерьер interior
Интурист Intourist
инфаркт heart attack
инфекционный/ая infectious
информация information
ипподром race course
Ирландия Ireland
ирландский/ая *adj* Irish
искра spark
искуственный/ая artificial
искусство art; **прикладное искусство** arts and crafts
исповедь confession
исполнитель/ница *m/f* performer
исследовательский/ая *adj* research
истина truth
исторический/ая historical
история history, story
итог result
июль July
июнь June

йога yoga
йод iodine

А	а	А
Б	б	Б
В	в	В
Г	г	Г
Д	д	Д
Е	е	Е
Ё	ё	Ё
Ж	ж	Ж
З	з	З
И	и	И
Й	й	Й
К	к	К
Л	л	Л
М	м	М
Н	н	Н
О	о	О
П	п	П
Р	р	Р
С	с	С
Т	т	Т
У	у	У
Ф	ф	Ф
Х	х	Х
Ц	ц	Ц
Ч	ч	Ч
Ш	ш	Ш
Щ	щ	Щ
Ъ	ъ	Ъ
Ы	ы	Ы
Ь	ь	Ь
Э	э	Э
Ю	ю	Ю
Я	я	Я

кабаре cabaret
кабинет office; study *(room)*
Кавказ Caucasus
кадры personnel
каждый/ая every
какао cocoa
календарь calendar
калькулятор calculator
камбала plaice
камень stone
камера chamber; cell; **автоматическая камера хранения** left-luggage locker
канал canal; channel
каникулы vacation
канцелярия stationery
капля drop
капуста cabbage; **кислая капуста** sauerkraut **цветная капуста** cauliflower; **брюссельская капуста** Brussels sprouts; **морская капуста** laminaria
каракуль Persian lamb *(fur)*
карандаш pencil; **цветной карандаш** crayon
карантин quarantine
карат carat
карикатура caricature
карман pocket
карманный/ая *adj* pocket; **карманный словарь** pocket dictionary
карнавал carnival
карта map; **карта-схема города** town map
карты playing cards
картина painting
картинная галерея art gallery
картофель potatoes
картошка potatoes
карточка card; **проездная карточка** transcard; season ticket; **фотокарточка** photograph
карусель merry-go-round

А	а	А
Б	б	Б
В	в	В
Г	г	Г
Д	д	Д
Е	е	Е
Ё	ё	Ё
Ж	ж	Ж
З	з	З
И	и	И
Й	й	Й
К	к	К
Л	л	Л
М	м	М
Н	н	Н
О	о	О
П	п	П
Р	р	Р
С	с	С
Т	т	Т
У	у	У
Ф	ф	Ф
Х	х	Х
Ц	ц	Ц
Ч	ч	Ч
Ш	ш	Ш
Щ	щ	Щ
Ъ	ъ	Ъ
Ы	ы	Ы
Ь	ь	Ь
Э	э	Э
Ю	ю	Ю
Я	я	Я

касса cash desk; till; **билетная касса** booking office; **театральная касса** box office; **касса-автомат** slot machine

кассета cassette

кассир cashier

кастрюля pan; pot

катание driving; riding

катер speedboat

кафе café

кафетерий cafeteria

качели swings

качество quality

каша pudding; **манная каша** semolina pudding; **гречневая каша** buckwheat pudding; **рисовая каша** rice pudding; **овсяная каша** porridge

каюта berth.

кают-компания passenger lounge *(on ship)*

квартира flat

квас kvas *(fermented bread drink)*

квитанция receipt

кекс fruitcake

кемпинг camp site

керамика ceramics

кета keta salmon

килограмм (кг) kilo

километр (км) kilometre

киностудия film studio

кино(театр) cinema

киоск kiosk; newsstand

Китай China

кладбище cemetery; burial ground

класс class

классический/ая classical

клей glue

клетка cage

клуб club

клубника strawberries

А	а	А
Б	б	Б
В	в	В
Г	г	Г
Д	д	Д
Е	е	Е
Ё	ё	Ё
Ж	ж	Ж
З	з	З
И	и	И
Й	й	Й
К	к	К
Л	л	Л
М	м	М
Н	н	Н
О	о	О
П	п	П
Р	р	Р
С	с	С
Т	т	Т
У	у	У
Ф	ф	Ф
Х	х	Х
Ц	ц	Ц
Ч	ч	Ч
Ш	ш	Ш
Щ	щ	Щ
Ъ	ъ	Ъ
Ы	ы	Ы
Ь	ь	Ь
Э	э	Э
Ю	ю	Ю
Я	я	Я

клюква cranberries

ключ key

книга book; **жалобная книга** complaints book; **Дом Книги** House of Books *(bookshop)*

кнопка drawing pin

ковер carpet

когда when

кожгалантерея leather goods

коктейль cocktail

колбаса sausage; **колбаса твердого копчения** salami; **вареная колбаса** boiled sausage

колготки tights

колесо wheel; **ремонт колес** wheel repairs

количество amount; quantity

коллекция collection

колхоз collective farm

кольцо ring

комар mosquito

комедия comedy; **театр комедии** comedy theatre

комиссионный магазин second-hand shop

коммунизм communism

комната room

комплект complete set

компостер ticket punch machine

компьютер computer

конверт envelope

кондитерский/ая *adj* confectionery

конец end

конкурс competition

консервы tinned food

конституция constitution *(political)*

контракт contract

контроль control

конфеты sweets

концерт concert

коньяк cognac; brandy

А	а	А
Б	б	Б
В	в	В
Г	г	Г
Д	д	Д
Е	е	Е
Ё	ё	Ё
Ж	ж	Ж
З	з	З
И	и	И
Й	й	Й
К	к	К
Л	л	Л
М	м	М
Н	н	Н
О	о	О
П	п	П
Р	р	Р
С	с	С
Т	т	Т
У	у	У
Ф	ф	Ф
Х	х	Х
Ц	ц	Ц
Ч	ч	Ч
Ш	ш	Ш
Щ	щ	Щ
Ъ	ъ	Ъ
Ы	ы	Ы
Ь	ь	Ь
Э	э	Э
Ю	ю	Ю
Я	я	Я

конь horse

коньки skates

кооператив co-operative

копия copy

копчености smoked food

корабль ship; vessel

коралл coral

корова cow

коротковолновый/ая short-wave

косметика cosmetics

косметический/ая cosmetic; **косметический салон**
  beauty parlour

костюм suit

кот tomcat

котлета burger; rissole

котлетная canteen

кофе coffee; **кофе в зернах** coffee beans; **молотый кофе**
  ground coffee; **кофеварка** coffee maker

кофта cardigan

кошелек purse

кошка cat *(female)*

красивый/ая beautiful

краска paint; dye; **акварельная краска** watercolour;
  масляная краска oil paint

красный/ая red

красота beauty

краткий/ая brief; short

кредит credit

крем cream

Кремль Kremlin

крепдешин crepe de Chine

крепкий/ая strong; firm

крещение baptism

критика criticism

кровать bed

кровь blood

А	а	А
Б	б	Б
В	в	В
Г	г	Г
Д	д	Д
Е	е	Е
Ё	ё	Ё
Ж	ж	Ж
З	з	З
И	и	И
Й	й	Й
К	к	К
Л	л	Л
М	м	М
Н	н	Н
О	о	О
П	п	П
Р	р	Р
С	с	С
Т	т	Т
У	у	У
Ф	ф	Ф
Х	х	Х
Ц	ц	Ц
Ч	ч	Ч
Ш	ш	Ш
Щ	щ	Щ
Ъ	ъ	Ъ
Ы	ы	Ы
Ь	ь	Ь
Э	э	Э
Ю	ю	Ю
Я	я	Я

КРУ – ЛЕГ

круглый/ая round
кружево lace *(fabric)*
крупа cereal
крупный/ая big; large-scale
крыло wing
Крым Crimea
крыша roof
куда where (to)
кукла doll; puppet
кукольный театр puppet theatre
кулинария food shop; delicatessen
культтовары leisure goods
культура culture
кунсткамера chamber of curiosities
купальник swimsuit
купаться to swim; **купаться запрещено! опасно!** no swimming! danger!
купе compartment *(train)*
купля-продажа buying and selling
курить to smoke; **не курить!** no smoking!
курица chicken
курорт health resort
курс(ы) course(s)
куртка jacket; anorak
кухня kitchen

лаванда lavender
лавина avalanche
лагерь camp
лампа lamp
лампочка light bulb
ларек stall
лауреат prize winner
лебедь swan
левый/ая left
легкий/ая light; easy

А	а	А
Б	б	Б
В	в	В
Г	г	Г
Д	д	Д
Е	е	Е
Ё	ё	Ё
Ж	ж	Ж
З	з	З
И	и	И
Й	й	Й
К	к	К
Л	л	Л
М	м	М
Н	н	Н
О	о	О
П	п	П
Р	р	Р
С	с	С
Т	т	Т
У	у	У
Ф	ф	Ф
Х	х	Х
Ц	ц	Ц
Ч	ч	Ч
Ш	ш	Ш
Щ	щ	Щ
Ъ	ъ	Ъ
Ы	ы	Ы
Ь	ь	Ь
Э	э	Э
Ю	ю	Ю
Я	я	Я

легковой/ая *adj* passenger; **легковая машина** motor car
лед ice
леденец lollypop
ледокол icebreaker
лезвие blade
лекарственный/ая medicinal; **лекарственные травы** medicinal herbs
лекарство medicine; drug
лен linen
лента ribbon
лес forest
лестница stairs; ladder
летний/ая *adj* summer
лето summer
лечение medical treatment
ликер liqueur
лимон lemon
лиса fox
лист leaf; sheet *(paper)*
литература literature
лифт lift
лифчик bra
лихорадка fever
лицей lyceum
лицо face
лодка boat
лодочный/ая *adj* boat; **лодочная станция** boat hire; pier
ложа box *(theatre)*
ложка spoon
лозунг slogan
лосось salmon
лосьон lotion
лотерея lottery
лотерейный билет lottery ticket
лошадь horse
лук onion

А	а	А
Б	б	Б
В	в	В
Г	г	Г
Д	д	Д
Е	е	Е
Ё	ё	Ё
Ж	ж	Ж
З	з	З
И	и	И
Й	й	Й
К	к	К
Л	л	Л
М	м	М
Н	н	Н
О	о	О
П	п	П
Р	р	Р
С	с	С
Т	т	Т
У	у	У
Ф	ф	Ф
Х	х	Х
Ц	ц	Ц
Ч	ч	Ч
Ш	ш	Ш
Щ	щ	Щ
Ъ	ъ	Ъ
Ы	ы	Ы
Ь	ь	Ь
Э	э	Э
Ю	ю	Ю
Я	я	Я

луна moon
лыжи skis
любовь love
люди people
люкс de luxe; first class

магазин shop
магнитофон tape recorder
мазь ointment
май May
майка vest; t-shirt
майонез mayonnaise
малахит malachite *(stone)*
маленький/ая small; little
малина raspberries
мало little; not enough
мальчик boy
мама mother
манеж riding school; arena
маникюр manicure
маргарин margarine
маринованный/ая pickled
марка postage stamp; trade mark; mark *(money)*
мармелад fruit jelly
март March
маршрут route
маршрутное такси minibus; fixed-rate taxi
маска mask
масленка butter dish
маслины olives
масло butter; oil; **подсолнечное масло** sunflower oil;
   растительное масло vegetable oil; **сливочное масло**
   butter; **оливковое масло** olive oil
массаж massage
мастерская workshop
материя fabric

А	а	А
Б	б	Б
В	в	В
Г	г	Г
Д	д	Д
Е	е	Е
Ё	ё	Ё
Ж	ж	Ж
З	з	З
И	и	И
Й	й	Й
К	к	К
Л	л	Л
М	м	М
Н	н	Н
О	о	О
П	п	П
Р	р	Р
С	с	С
Т	т	Т
У	у	У
Ф	ф	Ф
Х	х	Х
Ц	ц	Ц
Ч	ч	Ч
Ш	ш	Ш
Щ	щ	Щ
Ъ	ъ	Ъ
Ы	ы	Ы
Ь	ь	Ь
Э	э	Э
Ю	ю	Ю
Я	я	Я

матовый/ая dull; mat

матрас mattress

матрешка matroshka (wooden doll)

матрос sailor

матч match (game)

мать mother

машина machine; car

маяк lighthouse

мебель furniture

мебельный магазин furniture shop

мед honey

медаль medal

медведь bear

медикаменты medicines; drugs

медпомощь medical aid

медпункт first-aid post

медсестра nurse

между between

междугородный/ая inter-city; **междугородный телефон** inter-city telephone line

мелодия melody

мелочь change (money)

мельхиор sterling silver

мемориал memorial; **мемориал жертвам войны** war memorial

меню menu

мера measure

месса mass (religious)

место place; seat; **места для пассажиров с детьми и инвалидов** seats for passengers with babies and for invalids

месяц month

метр (м) metre

метрдотель head waiter

метро (М) underground; Metro

меха fur

меховой/ая adj fur; **меховые изделия** fur goods

А	а	А
Б	б	Б
В	в	В
Г	г	Г
Д	д	Д
Е	е	Е
Ё	ё	Ё
Ж	ж	Ж
З	з	З
И	и	И
Й	й	Й
К	к	К
Л	л	Л
М	м	М
Н	н	Н
О	о	О
П	п	П
Р	р	Р
С	с	С
Т	т	Т
У	у	У
Ф	ф	Ф
Х	х	Х
Ц	ц	Ц
Ч	ч	Ч
Ш	ш	Ш
Щ	щ	Щ
Ъ	ъ	Ъ
Ы	ы	Ы
Ь	ь	Ь
Э	э	Э
Ю	ю	Ю
Я	я	Я

милиция militia; police
миллион million
миндаль almond
министерство (Мин) ministry
министр minister
минута minute
мир world; peace
мирный/ая peaceful; peace-
мнение opinion
много a lot; many
многоуважаемый/ая respected; dear (in letter)
мода fashion; **Дом мод** fashion house; **журнал мод** fashion magazine
модель model
мозаика mosaic
мокрый/ая wet; moist
молебен public prayer; service
молитва prayer
молодой/ая adj young
молоко milk
молочный/ая adj dairy; milk
монета coin
монпасье fruit drops (sweets)
море sea
морковь carrots
мороженое ice cream; **кафе-мороженое** ice-cream parlour
Москва Moscow
морской/ая adj sea; naval; **морской вокзал** seaport
мост bridge
мотор engine
мотоцикл motorcycle
мохер mohair
мощность horsepower (engine)
муж husband
мужской/ая men's; male

А	а	А
Б	б	Б
В	в	В
Г	г	Г
Д	д	Д
Е	е	Е
Ё	ё	Ё
Ж	ж	Ж
З	з	З
И	и	И
Й	й	Й
К	к	К
Л	л	Л
М	м	М
Н	н	Н
О	о	О
П	п	П
Р	р	Р
С	с	С
Т	т	Т
У	у	У
Ф	ф	Ф
Х	х	Х
Ц	ц	Ц
Ч	ч	Ч
Ш	ш	Ш
Щ	щ	Щ
Ъ	ъ	Ъ
Ы	ы	Ы
Ь	ь	Ь
Э	э	Э
Ю	ю	Ю
Я	я	Я

музей museum
музыка music
мука flour
мультфильм animated cartoon
мусор rubbish; litter
мы we
мыло soap; **туалетное мыло** toilet soap
мясо meat; **мясопродукты** meat products
мятный/ая mint-flavoured

наводнение flood
награда reward
наливка fruit liqueur; brandy
налог tax
напиток drink; beverage; **спиртные напитки** wines and spirits; **крепкие напитки** spirits; **безалкогольные напитки** soft drinks
наркоман drug addict
народ people
население population; inhabitants
наука science
научный/ая scientific
национальность nationality
начало beginning
начальник boss
наш our; ours
не not
небо sky
невеста bride; fiancée
неделя week
некурящий/ая non-smoking
нет no
нефрит jade (stone)
нефть oil (mineral)
новинка novelty; new product
новость news

А	а	А
Б	б	Б
В	в	В
Г	г	Г
Д	д	Д
Е	е	Е
Ё	ё	Ё
Ж	ж	Ж
З	з	З
И	и	И
Й	й	Й
К	к	К
Л	л	Л
М	м	М
Н	н	Н
О	о	О
П	п	П
Р	р	Р
С	с	С
Т	т	Т
У	у	У
Ф	ф	Ф
Х	х	Х
Ц	ц	Ц
Ч	ч	Ч
Ш	ш	Ш
Щ	щ	Щ
Ъ	ъ	Ъ
Ы	ы	Ы
Ь	ь	Ь
Э	э	Э
Ю	ю	Ю
Я	я	Я

НОВ – ОВО

новый/ая new; **Новый Год** New Year

нож knife

ножницы scissors

номер number; size; hotel room

норка mink

нос nose

носки socks

ночной/ая *adj* night; **ночной бар** night club

ночь night

ноябрь November

нырять to dive; **нырять запрещено!** no diving!

няня nanny

обед lunch; lunchbreak

обзорный/ая *adj* general; **обзорная экскурсия** sightseeing tour

область region

обмен exchange; **пункт обмена валюты** currency exchange point; **обменный пункт** exchange point

оборона defence

образец sample

образование education

обряд rite; ceremony; **свадебный обряд** wedding ceremony

обслуживание service; **самообслуживание** self-service

обувной отдел/магазин shoe department/shop

обувь footwear

общежитие hostel; hall of residence

общепит public catering

общество society

общий/ая common

объединение association

объезд detour

объявление advertisement

обязательный/ая compulsory

овощи vegetables

А	а	А
Б	б	Б
В	в	В
Г	г	Г
Д	д	Д
Е	е	Е
Ё	ё	Ё
Ж	ж	Ж
З	з	З
И	и	И
Й	й	Й
К	к	К
Л	л	Л
М	м	М
Н	н	Н
О	о	О
П	п	П
Р	р	Р
С	с	С
Т	т	Т
У	у	У
Ф	ф	Ф
Х	х	Х
Ц	ц	Ц
Ч	ч	Ч
Ш	ш	Ш
Щ	щ	Щ
Ъ	ъ	Ъ
Ы	ы	Ы
Ь	ь	Ь
Э	э	Э
Ю	ю	Ю
Я	я	Я

овсянка oats

огнетушитель fire extinguisher

огонь fire; flame

огурец cucumber

одежда clothes

одеколон eau-de-Cologne

одеяло blanket; quilt

однокомнатный/ая one-roomed

океан ocean

окно window

окорок gammon

октябрь October

оладьи dropscones

оливки olives

омар lobster

омлет omelette

он he

она she

они they

оно it

ООН United Nations Organization

опасно! danger!

опасный/ая dangerous; **опасная зона!** dangerous area!

опера opera; **Театр Оперы и Балета** Opera and Ballet Theatre

оперетта operetta

оперный/ая adj opera; **Большой Оперный** Bolshoi Opera Theatre; **Малый Оперный** Malii Opera Theatre

оплата payment

опоздавший/ая adj latecomer

оптика optician

оранжевый/ая adj orange (colour)

организация organization

орден order

орех nut; **кокосовый орех** coconut; **лесной орех** hazelnut; **мускатный орех** nutmeg

А	а	А
Б	б	Б
В	в	В
Г	г	Г
Д	д	Д
Е	е	Е
Ё	ё	Ё
Ж	ж	Ж
З	з	З
И	и	И
Й	й	Й
К	к	К
Л	л	Л
М	м	М
Н	н	Н
О	о	О
П	п	П
Р	р	Р
С	с	С
Т	т	Т
У	у	У
Ф	ф	Ф
Х	х	Х
Ц	ц	Ц
Ч	ч	Ч
Ш	ш	Ш
Щ	щ	Щ
Ъ	ъ	Ъ
Ы	ы	Ы
Ь	ь	Ь
Э	э	Э
Ю	ю	Ю
Я	я	Я

оркестр orchestra; **оркестр русских народных инструментов** Russian folk band

оружие arm; weapon

Оружейная палата Armoury (in Kremlin)

осветительные приборы lighting appliance

осень autumn

осетр(ина) sturgeon

осмотр examination; inspection; **тех(нический)осмотр** MOT

оставлять to leave; to abandon; **не оставляйте вещи без присмотра!** don't leave your luggage unattended!

остановка stop

осторожно! look out!; **осторожно, ступеньки!** mind the step!

отбор selection

ответ answer

ответственный/ая responsible

отдел department; section

отдых rest; **дом отдыха** holiday home

отель hotel

отец father

отечественный/ая adj national

отъезд departure (for train)

официант/ка waiter/waitress

оформление official registration

охота hunting

оценка estimate; evaluation

очень very

очередь queue; line

очки glasses; spectacles

падать to fall; to drop

палата chamber; ward; **Грановитая палата** The Faceted Hall (in Kremlin)

палатка tent

палец finger; toe

палка stick

А	а	А
Б	б	Б
В	в	В
Г	г	Г
Д	д	Д
Е	е	Е
Ё	ё	Ё
Ж	ж	Ж
З	з	З
И	и	И
Й	й	Й
К	к	К
Л	л	Л
М	м	М
Н	н	Н
О	о	О
П	п	П
Р	р	Р
С	с	С
Т	т	Т
У	у	У
Ф	ф	Ф
Х	х	Х
Ц	ц	Ц
Ч	ч	Ч
Ш	ш	Ш
Щ	щ	Щ
Ъ	ъ	Ъ
Ы	ы	Ы
Ь	ь	Ь
Э	э	Э
Ю	ю	Ю
Я	я	Я

палуба deck *(ship)*

пальто overcoat

памятник monument

память memory

пантомима pantomime

папа daddy

папиросы local brand of cigarettes

пара pair; couple

парад parade

парафин paraffin

парикмахерская hairdresser's; barber's

парилка sauna *(steam room)*

парк park; **Парк Культуры и Отдыха** amusement park; **автобусный парк** bus depot

паровоз steam engine

пароход steamer *(boat)*

партер stalls *(theatre)*

партия party; group

партнёр partner

парусный спорт sailing sport

парфюмерия perfumery

паспорт passport

пассаж arcade

пассажир/ка *m/f* passenger

паста paste; **зубная паста** toothpaste

Пасха Easter

пачка packet; pack

паштет pâté

паюсная икра pressed caviar

педикюр pedicure; chiropody

пейзаж view; landscape

пекарня bakery

пельмени pelmeni *(Siberian meat dumplings)*

пельменная snack bar serving pelmeni

пенсионер/ка *m/f* pensioner

пенсия pension

А	а	А
Б	б	Б
В	в	В
Г	г	Г
Д	д	Д
Е	е	Е
Ё	ё	Ё
Ж	ж	Ж
З	з	З
И	и	И
Й	й	Й
К	к	К
Л	л	Л
М	м	М
Н	н	Н
О	о	О
П	п	П
Р	р	Р
С	с	С
Т	т	Т
У	у	У
Ф	ф	Ф
Х	х	Х
Ц	ц	Ц
Ч	ч	Ч
Ш	ш	Ш
Щ	щ	Щ
Ъ	ъ	Ъ
Ы	ы	Ы
Ь	ь	Ь
Э	э	Э
Ю	ю	Ю
Я	я	Я

первый/ая first

переводить to translate; to interpret

переводчик translator; interpreter

переговорный пункт trunkcall station

переговоры talks; negotiations

перегрузка overload

переезд level crossing

перерыв break; intermission; **перерыв на обед** lunchbreak

перестройка perestroika; reorganization

переулок side street; lane

переучет stocktaking

переход pedestrian crossing; transition; **подземный переход** underground crossing

перец pepper

перламутр mother-of-pearl

перманент perm

персик peach

персиковый сок peach juice

перцовка pepper vodka

перчатки gloves

песня song

песок sand; **сахарный песок** granulated sugar

Петр Великий Peter the Great

петрушка parsley

печенье pastry; biscuit

пешеходный/ая *adj* pedestrian

пианино piano

пивной бар beer hall; pub

пиво beer

пикник picnic

пирог pie

пирожковая snack bar serving patties

пирожное pastries; cakes

писатель/ница *m/f* writer; author

писчебумажные принадлежности stationery

А	а	А
Б	б	Б
В	в	В
Г	г	Г
Д	д	Д
Е	е	Е
Ё	ё	Ё
Ж	ж	Ж
З	з	З
И	и	И
Й	й	Й
К	к	К
Л	л	Л
М	м	М
Н	н	Н
О	о	О
П	п	П
Р	р	Р
С	с	С
Т	т	Т
У	у	У
Ф	ф	Ф
Х	х	Х
Ц	ц	Ц
Ч	ч	Ч
Ш	ш	Ш
Щ	щ	Щ
Ъ	ъ	Ъ
Ы	ы	Ы
Ь	ь	Ь
Э	э	Э
Ю	ю	Ю
Я	я	Я

письмо letter; **заказное письмо** registered letter

питание nourishment; food; **детское питание** baby food

пить to drink

питьевая вода drinking water

пища food

плавание swimming

плавки swimming trunks

плакат poster

пламя flame

план plan

планета planet

планетарий planetarium

пластинки records; LPs

пластырь plaster *(sticking)*

плата fee; fare

платина platinum

платить to pay

платный/ая *adj* requiring payment

платок headscarf; **носовой платок** handkerchief

платформа platform

платье dress; **готовое платье** clothes

плацкартный/ая with reserved seats

плащ raincoat

пленка film *(for camera)*; **магнитофонная пленка** tape

плечики coat hanger

плечо shoulder

плита cooker

плитка tile; cooker; bar *(chocolate)*

плов pilau rice

плод fruit

плодоовощной магазин greengrocer's

пломбир ice cream

плотина dam

плохой/ая bad

площадь square *(in town)*

пляж beach

А	а	А
Б	б	Б
В	в	В
Г	г	Г
Д	д	Д
Е	е	Е
Ё	ё	Ё
Ж	ж	Ж
З	з	З
И	и	И
Й	й	Й
К	к	К
Л	л	Л
М	м	М
Н	н	Н
О	о	О
П	п	П
Р	р	Р
С	с	С
Т	т	Т
У	у	У
Ф	ф	Ф
Х	х	Х
Ц	ц	Ц
Ч	ч	Ч
Ш	ш	Ш
Щ	щ	Щ
Ъ	ъ	Ъ
Ы	ы	Ы
Ь	ь	Ь
Э	э	Э
Ю	ю	Ю
Я	я	Я

пляска dancing; **ансамбль песни и пляски** folk ensemble

повар cook; **шеф-повар** chef; **поваренная книга** cook book

повесть novel

повидло jam

поворот turning

погода weather

подарок present; gift

поделка handmade article

поднос tray

пододеяльник duvet cover

подушка pillow

подъезд entrance

поезд train; **скорый поезд** fast train; **поезда дальнего следования** long-distance trains

поездка journey

пожар fire

поздравительный/ая congratulatory; **поздравительная открытка** congratulations card

показ show; demonstration

поколение generation

покупатель buyer; consumer

покупка purchase

пол- half-

полдень midday; noon

поле field

полет flight

поликлиника health centre

полка shelf; berth

полотенце towel

полотно linen

полупальто short coat

полуфинал semi final

полушерсть wool mixture

пользование use

помада lipstick

А	а	А
Б	б	Б
В	в	В
Г	г	Г
Д	д	Д
Е	е	Е
Ё	ё	Ё
Ж	ж	Ж
З	з	З
И	и	И
Й	й	Й
К	к	К
Л	л	Л
М	м	М
Н	н	Н
О	о	О
П	п	П
Р	р	Р
С	с	С
Т	т	Т
У	у	У
Ф	ф	Ф
Х	х	Х
Ц	ц	Ц
Ч	ч	Ч
Ш	ш	Ш
Щ	щ	Щ
Ъ	ъ	Ъ
Ы	ы	Ы
Ь	ь	Ь
Э	э	Э
Ю	ю	Ю
Я	я	Я

помидор tomato

помощь help; **скорая помощь** ambulance

пончик doughnut

порошок powder

порт port; harbour

портрет portrait

портфель briefcase

по-русски in Russian; **вы говорите по-русски?** do you speak Russian?

порядок order; **в порядке очереди** in turn

посадка boarding

поселок settlement

посетитель/ница *m/f* visitor

пословица proverb

пособие manual

посол ambassador

постановка play; performance

постель bed; **постельное белье** bed linen; **постельные принадлежности** bedding

посторонний/яя outsider; **посторонним вход воспрещен!** no entry!

посуда tableware

посудный магазин crockery shop

посылка parcel

почетный/ая honourable

почта post office; **почтамт** head post office

почтовый/ая postal; **почтовый ящик** letterbox; **почтовая марка** stamp; **почтовое отделение** local post office

пошлина duty

поэзия poetry

правда truth

правило rule; **правила уличного движения** highway code

право right to

православный/ая orthodox

правый/ая right

А	а	А
Б	б	Б
В	в	В
Г	г	Г
Д	д	Д
Е	е	Е
Ё	ё	Ё
Ж	ж	Ж
З	з	З
И	и	И
Й	й	Й
К	к	К
Л	л	Л
М	м	М
Н	н	Н
О	о	О
П	п	П
Р	р	Р
С	с	С
Т	т	Т
У	у	У
Ф	ф	Ф
Х	х	Х
Ц	ц	Ц
Ч	ч	Ч
Ш	ш	Ш
Щ	щ	Щ
Ъ	ъ	Ъ
Ы	ы	Ы
Ь	ь	Ь
Э	э	Э
Ю	ю	Ю
Я	я	Я

праздник holiday

прачечная laundry

предмет object; article; **предметы первой необходимости** basic commodities; **предметы ширпотреба** consumer goods

предприятие undertaking

председатель chairman

президент president

прейскурант price list

премьера first night

премьер-министр prime minister

прибор instrument; appliance

прибытие arrivals

привет greetings; **привет!** hi!

пригородный/ая suburban; **пригородные поезда** local trains

прием reception

прикладной/ая applied; artistic; **музей прикладного творчества** museum of applied arts

прилавок counter

прилет arrivals *(by air)*

прилетать to arrive *(by air)*

примерять to try on

примерочная fitting room

приморский курорт seaside resort

принадлежность accessory; equipment; **письменные принадлежности** stationery; **рыболовные принадлежности** fishing tackle; **туалетные принадлежности** toiletries

природа nature

пристань pier

прическа hairstyle

приятный/ая nice; pleasant

проблема problem

провоз transportation

провозить to transport

прогноз forecast

А	а	А
Б	б	Б
В	в	В
Г	г	Г
Д	д	Д
Е	е	Е
Ё	ё	Ё
Ж	ж	Ж
З	з	З
И	и	И
Й	й	Й
К	к	К
Л	л	Л
М	м	М
Н	н	Н
О	о	О
П	п	П
Р	р	Р
С	с	С
Т	т	Т
У	у	У
Ф	ф	Ф
Х	х	Х
Ц	ц	Ц
Ч	ч	Ч
Ш	ш	Ш
Щ	щ	Щ
Ъ	ъ	Ъ
Ы	ы	Ы
Ь	ь	Ь
Э	э	Э
Ю	ю	Ю
Я	я	Я

программа programme

продавец salesman

продажа selling

продовольственный/ая *adj* food

продмаг grocery store

продукт product; foodstuff; **молочные продукты** dairy produce

продуктовый магазин foodstore

проезд passage; **проезд закрыт!** no entry! *(cars)*

прокат hire; **прокат лыж** skis for hire

промтовары manufactured goods

промышленность industry

прописка residence permit

пропуск pass; permit

проспект prospect; avenue

простой/ая simple

простыня bedsheet

просьба request; **просьба соблюдать тишину!** silence please!

против against

противозачаточный/ая *adj* contraceptive

противостолбнячный/ая anti-tetanus

профессиональный/ая professional

профсоюз trade union

прохладительный/ая refreshing; **прохладительные напитки** soft drinks

проход passage; **прохода нет!** no entry *(pedestrians)*

прощальный/ая *adj* farewell

проявлять to show; to develop *(film)*

пряжа yarn

прямой/ая straight; direct

пряник spice cake

птица bird; poultry

публичный/ая public

пудра powder; **сахарная пудра** icing sugar

А	а	А
Б	б	Б
В	в	В
Г	г	Г
Д	д	Д
Е	е	Е
Ё	ё	Ё
Ж	ж	Ж
З	з	З
И	и	И
Й	й	Й
К	к	К
Л	л	Л
М	м	М
Н	н	Н
О	о	О
П	п	П
Р	р	Р
С	с	С
Т	т	Т
У	у	У
Ф	ф	Ф
Х	х	Х
Ц	ц	Ц
Ч	ч	Ч
Ш	ш	Ш
Щ	щ	Щ
Ъ	ъ	Ъ
Ы	ы	Ы
Ь	ь	Ь
Э	э	Э
Ю	ю	Ю
Я	я	Я

пузырь bubble

пуловер pullover

пункт point; **мед(ицинский) пункт** dispensary; **конечный пункт** terminus

пустыня desert

пусть let (it) be!

путеводитель guidebook

путешествие journey; voyage

путь way; track

пушнина fur

пчелиный/ая *adj* bees

пшеничный/ая *adj* wheat

пьеса play

пюре purée; **картофельное пюре** mashed potatoes

работа work

работать to work; **не работает** closed; does not work

радио radio

радиопередача radio transmission; programme

радуга rainbow

разговор conversation; **разговорник** phrase book

раздевалка cloakroom

размен exchange; change; **размен денег** change machine

размер size; dimensions

разрешение permit; permission

разряд category; sort; **первого разряда** first class

район region

рамка frame

ранний/ая early

раскопки excavations

расписание timetable; **расписание поездов** train timetable

распродажа sale

рассольник meat/fish soup with salted cucumbers

расстояние distance

А	а	А
Б	б	Б
В	в	В
Г	г	Г
Д	д	Д
Е	е	Е
Ё	ё	Ё
Ж	ж	Ж
З	з	З
И	и	И
Й	й	Й
К	к	К
Л	л	Л
М	м	М
Н	н	Н
О	о	О
П	п	П
Р	р	Р
С	с	С
Т	т	Т
У	у	У
Ф	ф	Ф
Х	х	Х
Ц	ц	Ц
Ч	ч	Ч
Ш	ш	Ш
Щ	щ	Щ
Ъ	ъ	Ъ
Ы	ы	Ы
Ь	ь	Ь
Э	э	Э
Ю	ю	Ю
Я	я	Я

расческа comb
ратуша town hall
рафинад sugar *(lumps)*
ребенок child
ревень rhubarb
ревизия inspection
революция revolution
регистратура registry
редакция editorial office
редис(ка) radish
режим regime; routine
режиссер director
резервировать to reserve
резиновый/ая *adj* rubber; **резиновая обувь** rubber
  footwear
резус-фактор rhesus factor
рейс № flight number; train number
река river
реклама advertising
религия religion
ремесло handicraft
ремонт repair; **ремонтная мастерская** repair shop
рентген x-ray
репа turnip
репертуар repertoire
репетиция rehearsal
репродукция reproduction *(painting, furniture)*
ресницы eyelashes
республика republic; **автономная республика**
  autonomous republic
рессоры suspension
реформа reform
рецепт recipe; prescription
речка small river
речь speech
решение decision

А	а	А
Б	б	Б
В	в	В
Г	г	Г
Д	д	Д
Е	е	Е
Ё	ё	Ё
Ж	ж	Ж
З	з	З
И	и	И
Й	й	Й
К	к	К
Л	л	Л
М	м	М
Н	н	Н
О	о	О
П	п	П
Р	р	Р
С	с	С
Т	т	Т
У	у	У
Ф	ф	Ф
Х	х	Х
Ц	ц	Ц
Ч	ч	Ч
Ш	ш	Ш
Щ	щ	Щ
Ъ	ъ	Ъ
Ы	ы	Ы
Ь	ь	Ь
Э	э	Э
Ю	ю	Ю
Я	я	Я

ржаной/ая *adj* rye
рис rice
рисование drawing
родина homeland
родители parents
родственник relative
Рождество Christmas
розетка socket
розовый/ая pink
роль role
роман novel
роскошь luxury
Россия Russia
рост height; growth
рот mouth
рубашка shirt; **ночная рубашка** nightdress
рубль rouble
рука hand; arm
рукавица mitten
румяна rouge; blusher
русский/ая *adj* Russian
русско-английский/ая *adj* Russian-English
ручка handle; pen; biro
ручной/ая *adj* hand; manual; tame *(animals)*; **ручной багаж** hand luggage; **ручная работа** handmade
рыба fish
рыбный/ая *adj* fish; **рыбный суп** fish soup
рынок market place; market
рюкзак rucksack
рюмка wine glass
ряд row
ряженка type of yoghurt

сад garden; orchard; **садовод** gardener; botanist
салат lettuce; salad
сало fat; lard

А	а	А
Б	б	Б
В	в	В
Г	г	Г
Д	д	Д
Е	е	Е
Ё	ё	Ё
Ж	ж	Ж
З	з	З
И	и	И
Й	й	Й
К	к	К
Л	л	Л
М	м	М
Н	н	Н
О	о	О
П	п	П
Р	р	Р
С	с	С
Т	т	Т
У	у	У
Ф	ф	Ф
Х	х	Х
Ц	ц	Ц
Ч	ч	Ч
Ш	ш	Ш
Щ	щ	Щ
Ъ	ъ	Ъ
Ы	ы	Ы
Ь	ь	Ь
Э	э	Э
Ю	ю	Ю
Я	я	Я

салон salon; **салон красоты** beauty parlour; художественный салон art shop

салфетка napkin; serviette

само- auto- ; self- ; **самовар** samovar; **самолет** airplane; **самообслуживание** self-service; **магазин самообслуживания** self-service store

самый/ая the most; the very

санаторий sanitorium

сани sledge

санитарный/ая sanitary; medical; **санитарный день** day off for cleaning

сантиметр (см) centimetre; tape measure

сапог boot

сапожный/ая *adj* shoe; **сапожная мастерская** shoe repair shop; **сапожная щетка** shoe brush

сарафан sundress

сардельки small sausages

сардина pilchard; sardine

сатира satire

сахар sugar

сахарный/ая *adj* sugar; **сахарный песок** granulated sugar; **сахарная пудра** icing sugar

сбер(егательная) касса savings bank

сборный/ая mixed; assembled; **сборная Советского Союза** National team

свадьба wedding

свежий/ая fresh

свекла beetroot

светильник lamp

светофор traffic lights

свеча candle

свидетельство certificate

свинина pork

свинья pig

свитер sweater

свобода freedom

свободный/ая free; easy

А	а	А
Б	б	Б
В	в	В
Г	г	Г
Д	д	Д
Е	е	Е
Ё	ё	Ё
Ж	ж	Ж
З	з	З
И	и	И
Й	й	Й
К	к	К
Л	л	Л
М	м	М
Н	н	Н
О	о	О
П	п	П
Р	р	Р
С	с	С
Т	т	Т
У	у	У
Ф	ф	Ф
Х	х	Х
Ц	ц	Ц
Ч	ч	Ч
Ш	ш	Ш
Щ	щ	Щ
Ъ	ъ	Ъ
Ы	ы	Ы
Ь	ь	Ь
Э	э	Э
Ю	ю	Ю
Я	я	Я

связь connection; communications; **отделение связи** post and telephone office

святой/ая holy; saint

священник priest

сгущеное молоко evaporated milk

сдача change *(money)*

сдоба fancy cakes; buns

сеанс performance *(cinema)*

себя (one)self; **от себя** push; **на себя** pull *(door)*

север north

сегодня today; **сегодня в продаже** today we sell...

сезон season

сейчас now

секретарь secretary

секс sex

секунда second; **секундомер** stopwatch

селедка salted herring

село village

сельский/ая rural; **сельское хозяйство** agriculture

сельдь herring

семечки sunflower seeds

семья family

сенат senate

сено hay

сентябрь September

сервиз dinner service

сердце heart

серебро silver

серый/ая grey

серьги earrings

сестра sister

Сибирь Siberia

сигара cigar

сигарета cigarette

сидеть to sit

сила strength; force

А	а	А
Б	б	Б
В	в	В
Г	г	Г
Д	д	Д
Е	е	Е
Ё	ё	Ё
Ж	ж	Ж
З	з	З
И	и	И
Й	й	Й
К	к	К
Л	л	Л
М	м	М
Н	н	Н
О	о	О
П	п	П
Р	р	Р
С	с	С
Т	т	Т
У	у	У
Ф	ф	Ф
Х	х	Х
Ц	ц	Ц
Ч	ч	Ч
Ш	ш	Ш
Щ	щ	Щ
Ъ	ъ	Ъ
Ы	ы	Ы
Ь	ь	Ь
Э	э	Э
Ю	ю	Ю
Я	я	Я

симфонический/ая symphonic
синагога synagogue
синий/яя navy blue
синтетика synthetic (material)
сироп syrup
система system
ситец printed cotton
сказка fairy tale
скалка rolling pin
скатерть tablecloth
скачки horse racing
сквер public garden
скидка reduction
склад storehouse
сковорода frying pan
сколько how much/many
скорый/ая fast; quick; **скорая помощь** ambulance; **скороговорка** tongue twister
скорость speed; gear
скрипка violin
скульптура sculpture
скумбрия mackerel
скупка buying up
слабый/ая weak
слава Богу! thank God!
славянин/славянка m/f Slav
славянский/ая Slavonic
сладкий/ая adj sweet
сласти sweet meats
слева to/on the left
сливки cream; **сбитые сливки** whipped cream
сливовый/ая adj plum; **сливовый сок** plum juice; **сливянка** plum brandy
словарь dictionary
слово word
сложный/ая complicated; complex

А	а	А
Б	б	Б
В	в	В
Г	г	Г
Д	д	Д
Е	е	Е
Ё	ё	Ё
Ж	ж	Ж
З	з	З
И	и	И
Й	й	Й
К	к	К
Л	л	Л
М	м	М
Н	н	Н
О	о	О
П	п	П
Р	р	Р
С	с	С
Т	т	Т
У	у	У
Ф	ф	Ф
Х	х	Х
Ц	ц	Ц
Ч	ч	Ч
Ш	ш	Ш
Щ	щ	Щ
Ъ	ъ	Ъ
Ы	ы	Ы
Ь	ь	Ь
Э	э	Э
Ю	ю	Ю
Я	я	Я

слон elephant
служащий/ая *m/f* office worker
служба service
смена change; shift
сметана soured cream
смех laughter
смородина currant
снасти tackle; **рыболовные снасти** fishing tackle
снег snow; **снегопад** snowfall
снотворное sleeping pill
собака dog
собор cathedral
собрание meeting; assembly
собственность property
совет council
советский/ая *adj* Soviet
сода soda
соединять to join; to unite
сок juice; **фруктовый сок** fruit juice
соска baby's dummy
сокращение reduction
солдат soldier
солидарность solidarity
солнце sun
солёный/ая salty
соль salt
солянка savoury fish/meat soup
сон sleep; dream
соревнование competition
сорочка shirt; blouse; **мужская сорочка** shirt; **женская сорочка** petticoat; **ночная сорочка** nightgown
сорт sort; quality; **высший сорт** best quality
сосиска frankfurter
сосисочная snack bar serving frankfurters
сотрудничество cooperation
соус sauce; dressing

А	а	А
Б	б	Б
В	в	В
Г	г	Г
Д	д	Д
Е	е	Е
Ё	ё	Ё
Ж	ж	Ж
З	з	З
И	и	И
Й	й	Й
К	к	К
Л	л	Л
М	м	М
Н	н	Н
О	о	О
П	п	П
Р	р	Р
С	с	С
Т	т	Т
У	у	У
Ф	ф	Ф
Х	х	Х
Ц	ц	Ц
Ч	ч	Ч
Ш	ш	Ш
Щ	щ	Щ
Ъ	ъ	Ъ
Ы	ы	Ы
Ь	ь	Ь
Э	э	Э
Ю	ю	Ю
Я	я	Я

сохранять to preserve

социалистический/ая *adj* socialist

союз union

спальня bedroom

спасательный/ая *adj* rescue

спасибо thanks

спать to sleep

спектакль play; performance

специя spice

спина back *(of body)*

спирт spirits; alcohol; **спиртные напитки** wines and spirits

спица knitting needle

спички matches

спорт sport

справа to/on the right

справка information; reference

справочник reference book

спутник companion; satellite

Средняя Азия Central Asia

срочный/ая urgent

стадион stadium

стакан tumbler; glass

станция station; **станция техобслуживания** service station *(for cars)*

стартер starter *(motor)*

старый/ая old

стекло glass; glassware

стерлинг sterling; **фунт (стерлингов)** pound *(sterling)*

стирка washing; **стирка белья** laundry service

стихи poetry

сто hundred

стоимость cost; price

стоить to cost

стол table; **адресный стол** address bureau

столица capital

А	а	А
Б	б	Б
В	в	В
Г	г	Г
Д	д	Д
Е	е	Е
Ё	ё	Ё
Ж	ж	Ж
З	з	З
И	и	И
Й	й	Й
К	к	К
Л	л	Л
М	м	М
Н	н	Н
О	о	О
П	п	П
Р	р	Р
С	с	С
Т	т	Т
У	у	У
Ф	ф	Ф
Х	х	Х
Ц	ц	Ц
Ч	ч	Ч
Ш	ш	Ш
Щ	щ	Щ
Ъ	ъ	Ъ
Ы	ы	Ы
Ь	ь	Ь
Э	э	Э
Ю	ю	Ю
Я	я	Я

СТО – ТВО

столовая canteen; dining hall
стоп stop; **стоп-кран** emergency brake *(bus, train, etc)*
сторона side
стоять to stand
страна country
страхование insurance
стрижка haircut
строительный/ая *adj* building
студент student
студень meat jelly; aspic
стул chair
сувенир souvenir
судак pikeperch
сумка bag
сумма amount
суп soup
сухой/ая dry
сухофрукты dried fruits
схема plan
сцена stage
счастливый/ая happy; lucky; **счастливого пути!** bon voyage!
счет bill
сын son
сыр cheese

табак tobacco
такси taxi; **стоянка такси** taxi rank
талон coupon; ticket
таможня customs; **таможенный досмотр** customs examination
танец dance
тапочки slippers
тарелка plate
тариф tariff
творог curd cheese

А	а	А
Б	б	Б
В	в	В
Г	г	Г
Д	д	Д
Е	е	Е
Ё	ё	Ё
Ж	ж	Ж
З	з	З
И	и	И
Й	й	Й
К	к	К
Л	л	Л
М	м	М
Н	н	Н
О	о	О
П	п	П
Р	р	Р
С	с	С
Т	т	Т
У	у	У
Ф	ф	Ф
Х	х	Х
Ц	ц	Ц
Ч	ч	Ч
Ш	ш	Ш
Щ	щ	Щ
Ъ	ъ	Ъ
Ы	ы	Ы
Ь	ь	Ь
Э	э	Э
Ю	ю	Ю
Я	я	Я

творческий/ая creative

театр theatre

театральный/ая *adj* theatre; **театральная касса** box office

телевидение television

телеграмма telegram; **телеграмма-молния** express telegram

телеграф telegraph

телекс telex

телефон telephone; **международный телефон** international telephone (lines); **телефон-автомат** public telephone

температура temperature

теннис tennis; **настольный теннис** table tennis

теплый/ая warm

терапевт doctor *(medical)*

термометр thermometer

термос vacuum flask

тетрадь exercise book

тетя aunt

техобслуживание maintenance

тишина silence

ткани fabrics

товары articles; goods; **продовольственные товары** foodstuffs; **промышленные товары** manufactured goods; **товары широкого потребления** consumer goods

товарищ comrade; friend

только only; merely

торговля trade

торжественный/ая solemn; gala

торжество celebration

тормоза brakes

торт cake

тост toast

трава grass

травма injury

трагедия tragedy

А	а	А
Б	б	Б
В	в	В
Г	г	Г
Д	д	Д
Е	е	Е
Ё	ё	Ё
Ж	ж	Ж
З	з	З
И	и	И
Й	й	Й
К	к	К
Л	л	Л
М	м	М
Н	н	Н
О	о	О
П	п	П
Р	р	Р
С	с	С
Т	т	Т
У	у	У
Ф	ф	Ф
Х	х	Х
Ц	ц	Ц
Ч	ч	Ч
Ш	ш	Ш
Щ	щ	Щ
Ъ	ъ	Ъ
Ы	ы	Ы
Ь	ь	Ь
Э	э	Э
Ю	ю	Ю
Я	я	Я

трамвай tram *(car)*
транспорт transport
требуются wanted; required
треска cod
трикотаж knitted wear
троллейбус trolleybus
труд labour; work
туалет toilet
туман fog
туризм tourism
турист/ка *m/f* tourist
туфли shoes
ты you *(singular, familiar)*
тюль curtain; lace
тянучка toffee

убор attire; **головной убор** headgear
уважаемый/ая respected; dear *(in letter)*
угол corner
уголь coal
ужас horror
ужин dinner; supper
указ decree; edict
указатель index; indicator
Украина Ukraine
украшение decoration; adornment
уксус vinegar
улица street
умелый/ая skilful
уметь to be able to
умный/ая clever; intelligent
универсальный/ая universal
универмаг department store
универсам self-service food store
университет university
упаковочный/ая packing

А	а	А
Б	б	Б
В	в	В
Г	г	Г
Д	д	Д
Е	е	Е
Ё	ё	Ё
Ж	ж	Ж
З	з	З
И	и	И
Й	й	Й
К	к	К
Л	л	Л
М	м	М
Н	н	Н
О	о	О
П	п	П
Р	р	Р
С	с	С
Т	т	Т
У	у	У
Ф	ф	Ф
Х	х	Х
Ц	ц	Ц
Ч	ч	Ч
Ш	ш	Ш
Щ	щ	Щ
Ъ	ъ	Ъ
Ы	ы	Ы
Ь	ь	Ь
Э	э	Э
Ю	ю	Ю
Я	я	Я

управленческий/ая administrative
упражнение exercise
ура! hooray!
урожай harvest
урок lesson
ускорение acceleration
условие condition; term
услуга service
успех success
устав charter; rules
устрица oyster
утка duck
утренний/яя *adj* morning
утро morning
утюг iron
ухо ear
уцененный/ая *adj* cut-price
участник participant
участок plot; section
учебник textbook
учебный/ая educational; training
учитель teacher
уют comfort

фабрика factory
фазан pheasant
факт fact
фамилия surname
фарфор china; porcelain
фасоль kidney beans
фаянс glazed pottery
февраль February
фен hair dryer
физкультура physical training
филармония philharmonic society
филиал branch *(shop)*

А	а	А
Б	б	Б
В	в	В
Г	г	Г
Д	д	Д
Е	е	Е
Ё	ё	Ё
Ж	ж	Ж
З	з	З
И	и	И
Й	й	Й
К	к	К
Л	л	Л
М	м	М
Н	н	Н
О	о	О
П	п	П
Р	р	Р
С	с	С
Т	т	Т
У	у	У
Ф	ф	Ф
Х	х	Х
Ц	ц	Ц
Ч	ч	Ч
Ш	ш	Ш
Щ	щ	Щ
Ъ	ъ	Ъ
Ы	ы	Ы
Ь	ь	Ь
Э	э	Э
Ю	ю	Ю
Я	я	Я

фильм film
фирма firm
фирменный/ая *adj* firm; **фирменное блюдо** speciality *(food)*
флот fleet; navy
фонтан fountain
форма form; uniform
фотоаппарат camera
фотография photography; photo
фотопленка photographic film
фрикадельки meat/fish balls
фрукты fruit
фуникулер cable railway
футбол football

халва halva *(sweet nut paste)*
хек hake
херес sherry
химчистка dry cleaner's
хлеб bread
хлопок cotton
хлопчатобумажный/ая *adj* cotton; **хлопчатобумажная ткань** cotton fabric
ходить to go; to walk
холодильник refrigerator
холодный/ая cold; chilled
холст canvas
хор chorus; choir
хороший/ая good; nice
хранение:камера хранения left-luggage office
хозяин host; owner
хозяйка hostess; owner
христианский/ая *adj* Christian
хроника chronical
хрупкий/ая fragile
хрусталь cut glass; crystal

художественный/ая artistic; **художественная литература** fiction; **художественный фильм** feature film; **художественное произведение** work of art
художник artist

царь tsar; king
цветной/ая coloured
цветы flowers
цель aim; target
цена price
ценный/ая valuable
центральный/ая central
церковь church
цирк circus
цыплёнок chick; **цыплёнок табака** fried young chicken

чай tea
час hour
частный/ая private
часы clock; watch
чашка cup
чебуреки meat pastry
чек cheque; receipt
чековый/ая *adj* cheque; **чековая книжка** cheque book
человек person; man
чемодан suitcase
черешня sweet cherries
чернила ink
Черное море Black Sea
черный/ая black
чеснок garlic
число number; date
чистка cleaning
чистый/ая clean
читальный/ая *adj* reading; **читальный зал** reading room

А	а	А
Б	б	Б
В	в	В
Г	г	Г
Д	д	Д
Е	е	Е
Ё	ё	Ё
Ж	ж	Ж
З	з	З
И	и	И
Й	й	Й
К	к	К
Л	л	Л
М	м	М
Н	н	Н
О	о	О
П	п	П
Р	р	Р
С	с	С
Т	т	Т
У	у	У
Ф	ф	Ф
Х	х	Х
Ц	ц	Ц
Ч	ч	Ч
Ш	ш	Ш
Щ	щ	Щ
Ъ	ъ	Ъ
Ы	ы	Ы
Ь	ь	Ь
Э	э	Э
Ю	ю	Ю
Я	я	Я

читать to read
член member
что what
чулки stockings

шампанское champagne
шампунь shampoo
шахматы chess
шашки draughts
шашлык shish kebab
шелк silk
шерсть wool
шеф-повар chef
шина tyre
шифр code
школа school
шлюпка boat; launch
шницель schnitzel; fillet *(pork or veal)*
шоколад chocolate
шоколадный/ая *adj* chocolate
шоколадка bar of chocolate
шоссе highway
Шотландия Scotland
шотландский/ая *adj* Scottish
шофер chauffeur; driver
шпинат spinach
штопор corkscrew
шторм gale
шуба fur coat
шутка joke
щелкунчик nutcracker
щетка brush
щи shchi *(cabbage soup)*

экзамен examination
экскурсия excursion

А	а	А
Б	б	Б
В	в	В
Г	г	Г
Д	д	Д
Е	е	Е
Ё	ё	Ё
Ж	ж	Ж
З	з	З
И	и	И
Й	й	Й
К	к	К
Л	л	Л
М	м	М
Н	н	Н
О	о	О
П	п	П
Р	р	Р
С	с	С
Т	т	Т
У	у	У
Ф	ф	Ф
Х	х	Х
Ц	ц	Ц
Ч	ч	Ч
Ш	ш	Ш
Щ	щ	Щ
Ъ	ъ	Ъ
Ы	ы	Ы
Ь	ь	Ь
Э	э	Э
Ю	ю	Ю
Я	я	Я

экскурсовод guide
экспонат exhibit
электрический/ая *adj* electric; **электричка** local train
электробытовой/ая electrical; **электробытовые приборы** electrical appliances
эмалированный/ая *adj* enamel
эмиграционный/ая *adj* emigration
энергия energy
энциклопедия encyclopaedia
Эрмитаж Hermitage
эстрадный/ая *adj* variety; **эстрадный концерт** variety show
этаж floor
этот/эта/это *m/f/nt* this
эти these

юбилей jubilee
ювелирный/ая *adj* jewellery
юг south
юмор humour
юность youth
юридический/ая legal
юрист lawyer

я I
яблоко apple
яд poison
язык tongue; language
яйцо egg
январь January
ярус tier; circle *(theatre)*
яхта yacht
яхт-клуб yacht club

А	а	А
Б	б	Б
В	в	В
Г	г	Г
Д	д	Д
Е	е	Е
Ё	ё	Ё
Ж	ж	Ж
З	з	З
И	и	И
Й	й	Й
К	к	К
Л	л	Л
М	м	М
Н	н	Н
О	о	О
П	п	П
Р	р	Р
С	с	С
Т	т	Т
У	у	У
Ф	ф	Ф
Х	х	Х
Ц	ц	Ц
Ч	ч	Ч
Ш	ш	Ш
Щ	щ	Щ
Ъ	ъ	Ъ
Ы	ы	Ы
Ь	ь	Ь
Э	э	Э
Ю	ю	Ю
Я	я	Я